GOVERNMENT PROCEDURES

FEDERAL DISCRETIONARY SPENDING AND BUDGET AUTHORITY

ELEMENTS AND TRENDS

GOVERNMENT PROCEDURES AND OPERATIONS

Additional books in this series can be found on Nova's website under the Series tab.

Additional e-books in this series can be found on Nova's website under the e-book tab.

FEDERAL DISCRETIONARY SPENDING AND BUDGET AUTHORITY

ELEMENTS AND TRENDS

GERALD A. GRASSO
EDITOR

New York

Copyright © 2014 by Nova Science Publishers, Inc.

For permission to use material from this book please contact us:
Telephone 631-231-7269; Fax 631-231-8175
Web Site: http://www.novapublishers.com

NOTICE TO THE READER

The Publisher has taken reasonable care in the preparation of this book, but makes no expressed or implied warranty of any kind and assumes no responsibility for any errors or omissions. No liability is assumed for incidental or consequential damages in connection with or arising out of information contained in this book. The Publisher shall not be liable for any special, consequential, or exemplary damages resulting, in whole or in part, from the readers' use of, or reliance upon, this material. Any parts of this book based on government reports are so indicated and copyright is claimed for those parts to the extent applicable to compilations of such works.

Independent verification should be sought for any data, advice or recommendations contained in this book. In addition, no responsibility is assumed by the publisher for any injury and/or damage to persons or property arising from any methods, products, instructions, ideas or otherwise contained in this publication.

This publication is designed to provide accurate and authoritative information with regard to the subject matter covered herein. It is sold with the clear understanding that the Publisher is not engaged in rendering legal or any other professional services. If legal or any other expert assistance is required, the services of a competent person should be sought. FROM A DECLARATION OF PARTICIPANTS JOINTLY ADOPTED BY A COMMITTEE OF THE AMERICAN BAR ASSOCIATION AND A COMMITTEE OF PUBLISHERS.

Additional color graphics may be available in the e-book version of this book.

Library of Congress Cataloging-in-Publication Data

ISBN: 978-1-63321-041-7

Published by Nova Science Publishers, Inc. † New York

CONTENTS

PREFACE

Discretionary spending covers the costs of the routine activities commonly associated with such federal government functions as running executive branch agencies, congressional offices and agencies, and international operations of the government. Essentially all spending on federal wages and salaries is discretionary. Discretionary spending also funds grants, purchases of equipment and other assets, and contractor services that support various federal programs and activities. Congress provides and controls discretionary funding through annual appropriations acts, which grant federal agencies the legal authority to obligate the U.S. government to make payments. Budget authority is the amount that can be legally obligated. Outlays are the payments made by the U.S. Treasury to satisfy those obligations. This book discusses trends in outlays. It also presents figures showing trends in discretionary budget authority as a percentage of GDP by subfunction within each of 17 budget function categories, using data from President Obama's FY2014 budget submission. It provides a starting point for discussions about spending trends.

Chapter 1 – Discretionary spending is provided and controlled through appropriations acts, which fund many of the activities commonly associated with such federal government functions as running executive branch agencies, congressional offices and agencies, and international operations of the government. Essentially all spending on federal wages and salaries is discretionary. Spending can be measured by budget authority (BA; what agencies can legally obligate the government to pay) or outlays (disbursements from the U.S. Treasury). This report mostly discusses trends in outlays.

Federal spending in fiscal year (FY) 2013 was just over a fifth (20.8%) of the U.S. economy, as measured as a share of gross domestic product (GDP), which is close to its average share since 1962. (Years denote federal fiscal years unless otherwise noted.) Discretionary spending accounted for 35% of total outlays in 2013 ($3,454 billion), well below mandatory spending's share (59% of outlays in 2013). Weak economic conditions in recent years as well as long-term demographic trends have increased spending on mandatory income support and retirement programs, while policy makers have acted to constrain the growth of discretionary spending. Net interest costs were 6.1% of federal outlays in 2013, but are projected to rise sharply.

Discretionary spending's share of total federal spending has fallen over time largely due to rapid growth of entitlement outlays. In 1962, discretionary spending accounted for 67% of total outlays and was the largest component of federal spending until the mid-1970s. Since then, discretionary spending as a share of federal outlays and as a share of GDP has fallen. Under current law projections, discretionary spending's share of GDP will fall to 5.5% in FY2023. Discretionary spending can be split into various categories to reflect broad national priorities or how federal spending decisions are made. In 1962, discretionary spending was 12.7% of GDP, with defense spending making up 9.3% of GDP. In 2012, discretionary spending was 7.6% of GDP, with defense spending (including war) totaling 3.9% of GDP. Defense spending can be divided between base budget and war expenditures, both of which grew sharply over the last decade. On average, defense outlays grew 6.8% per year in real terms from 2000 to 2010, while real nondefense discretionary outlays grew 5.6% per year. Discretionary spending has also been divided into security and non-security categories. Non-defense security spending, which rose sharply after 2001 and Hurricane Katrina in 2005, was 1.1% of GDP in 2013, nearly twice its pre-2001 level. Non-defense non-security outlays, which ranged between 3% and 3.5% of GDP since the mid-1980s, were 2.8% of GDP in 2013. Security spending was 5.0% of GDP in 2013.

The Budget Control Act of 2011 (BCA; P.L. 112-25) reintroduced statutory limits on spending by imposing a series of caps on discretionary BA from FY2012 through FY2021. The American Taxpayer Relief Act of 2012 (ATRA; P.L. 112-240) modified limits for FY2013 and FY2014. The FY2013 full-year funding bill (H.R. 933; P.L. 113-6) enacted March 26, 2013, conformed to those limits. The Bipartisan Budget Act (H.J.Res. 59; P.L. 113-67) also modified BCA limits for FY2014 and FY2015. On January 15, 2014, the House approved the Consolidated Appropriations Act, 2014 (H.R. 3547; P.L. 113-76) to provide funding within those limits for the rest of FY2014. The Senate passed it on the next day, and the President signed it into law the following day.

The direction of fiscal policy has been the focus of contention among macroeconomists. Some contend that more spending would help reduce high unemployment levels, while others call for imposing greater budgetary stringency. Over the long term, future growth in entitlement program outlays may put severe pressure on discretionary spending unless policy changes are enacted or federal revenues are increased.

Chapter 2 – This report provides a graphical overview of historical trends in discretionary budget authority (BA) from FY1976 through FY2012, preliminary estimates for FY2013 spending, and the levels consistent with the President's proposals for FY2014 through FY2018 using data from President Obama's FY2014 budget submission that was released on April 10, 2013. Spending caps and budget enforcement mechanisms established in the Budget Control Act of 2011 (P.L. 112-25; BCA) strongly affected the FY2013 and FY2014 budget cycles. Congress modified BCA caps at the beginning of January 2013 to scale down the size of discretionary spending reductions for FY2013 and in December 2013 to scale down the size of reductions slated for FY2014 and FY2015.

As the 113th Congress prepares to consider funding levels for FY2015 and beyond, past spending trends may help frame policy discussions. For example, rapid growth in national defense and other security spending in the past decade has played an important role in fiscal discussions. The American Recovery and Reinvestment Act of 2009 (P.L. 111-5; ARRA) funded sharp increases in spending on education, energy, and other areas. Since FY2010, however, base defense discretionary spending has essentially been held flat and non-defense discretionary spending has been reduced significantly. The base defense budget excludes war funding (Overseas Contingency Operations/Global War on Terror). This report provides a starting point for discussions about spending trends. Other CRS products analyze spending trends in specific functional areas.

Functional categories (e.g., national defense, agriculture, etc.) provide a means to compare federal funding for activities within broad policy areas that often cut across several federal agencies. Subfunction categories provide a finer division of funding levels within narrower policy areas. Budget function categories are used within the budget resolution and for other purposes, such as possible program cuts and tax expenditures. Three functions are omitted: (1) allowances, which contain items reflecting technical budget adjustments; (2) net interest, which by its nature is not discretionary spending; and (3) undistributed offsetting receipts, which are treated for federal budgetary purposes as negative budget authority.

Spending in this report is measured and illustrated in terms of discretionary budget authority as a percentage of gross domestic product (GDP). Measuring spending as a percentage of GDP in effect controls for inflation and population increases.

A flat line on such graphs indicates that spending in that category has been increasing at the same rate as overall economic growth. Graphs were updated to reflect the revisions to national income accounts released by the Department of Commerce's Bureau of Economic Analysis in July 2013.

Discretionary spending is provided and controlled through appropriations acts, which provide budget authority to federal agencies to fund many of the activities commonly associated with such federal government functions as running executive branch agencies, congressional offices and agencies, and international operations of the government. Essentially all spending on federal wages and salaries is discretionary.

Program administration costs for entitlement programs such as Social Security are generally funded by discretionary spending, while mandatory spending— not shown in figures presented in this report—generally funds the benefits provided through those programs. For some federal agencies, such as the Departments of Veterans Affairs and Transportation, the division of expenditures into discretionary and mandatory categories can be complex.

In: Federal Discretionary Spending ...   ISBN: 978-1-63321-041-7
Editor: Gerald A. Grasso   © 2014 Nova Science Publishers, Inc.

Chapter 1

TRENDS IN DISCRETIONARY SPENDING*

D. Andrew Austin

SUMMARY

Discretionary spending is provided and controlled through appropriations acts, which fund many of the activities commonly associated with such federal government functions as running executive branch agencies, congressional offices and agencies, and international operations of the government. Essentially all spending on federal wages and salaries is discretionary. Spending can be measured by budget authority (BA; what agencies can legally obligate the government to pay) or outlays (disbursements from the U.S. Treasury). This report mostly discusses trends in outlays.

Federal spending in fiscal year (FY) 2013 was just over a fifth (20.8%) of the U.S. economy, as measured as a share of gross domestic product (GDP), which is close to its average share since 1962. (Years denote federal fiscal years unless otherwise noted.) Discretionary spending accounted for 35% of total outlays in 2013 ($3,454 billion), well below mandatory spending's share (59% of outlays in 2013). Weak economic conditions in recent years as well as long-term demographic trends have increased spending on mandatory income support and retirement programs, while policy makers have acted to constrain the growth of discretionary spending. Net interest costs were 6.1% of federal outlays in 2013, but are projected to rise sharply.

---

* This is an edited, reformatted and augmented version of Congressional Research Service Publication, No. RL34424, dated January 24, 2014.

Discretionary spending's share of total federal spending has fallen over time largely due to rapid growth of entitlement outlays. In 1962, discretionary spending accounted for 67% of total outlays and was the largest component of federal spending until the mid-1970s. Since then, discretionary spending as a share of federal outlays and as a share of GDP has fallen. Under current law projections, discretionary spending's share of GDP will fall to 5.5% in FY2023. Discretionary spending can be split into various categories to reflect broad national priorities or how federal spending decisions are made. In 1962, discretionary spending was 12.7% of GDP, with defense spending making up 9.3% of GDP. In 2012, discretionary spending was 7.6% of GDP, with defense spending (including war) totaling 3.9% of GDP. Defense spending can be divided between base budget and war expenditures, both of which grew sharply over the last decade. On average, defense outlays grew 6.8% per year in real terms from 2000 to 2010, while real nondefense discretionary outlays grew 5.6% per year. Discretionary spending has also been divided into security and non-security categories. Non-defense security spending, which rose sharply after 2001 and Hurricane Katrina in 2005, was 1.1% of GDP in 2013, nearly twice its pre-2001 level. Non-defense non-security outlays, which ranged between 3% and 3.5% of GDP since the mid-1980s, were 2.8% of GDP in 2013. Security spending was 5.0% of GDP in 2013.

The Budget Control Act of 2011 (BCA; P.L. 112-25) reintroduced statutory limits on spending by imposing a series of caps on discretionary BA from FY2012 through FY2021. The American Taxpayer Relief Act of 2012 (ATRA; P.L. 112-240) modified limits for FY2013 and FY2014. The FY2013 full-year funding bill (H.R. 933; P.L. 113-6) enacted March 26, 2013, conformed to those limits. The Bipartisan Budget Act (H.J.Res. 59; P.L. 113-67) also modified BCA limits for FY2014 and FY2015. On January 15, 2014, the House approved the Consolidated Appropriations Act, 2014 (H.R. 3547; P.L. 113-76) to provide funding within those limits for the rest of FY2014. The Senate passed it on the next day, and the President signed it into law the following day.

The direction of fiscal policy has been the focus of contention among macroeconomists. Some contend that more spending would help reduce high unemployment levels, while others call for imposing greater budgetary stringency. Over the long term, future growth in entitlement program outlays may put severe pressure on discretionary spending unless policy changes are enacted or federal revenues are increased.

WHAT DOES DISCRETIONARY SPENDING INCLUDE?

Discretionary spending covers the costs of the routine activities commonly associated with such federal government functions as running executive branch agencies, congressional offices and agencies, and international operations of the government.[1] Essentially all spending on federal wages and salaries is discretionary.[2] Discretionary spending also funds grants, purchases of equipment and other assets, and contractor services that support various federal programs and activities.

Congress provides and controls discretionary funding through annual appropriations acts, which grant federal agencies the legal authority to obligate the U.S. government to make payments. Budget authority (BA) is the amount that can be legally obligated. Outlays are the payments made by the U.S. Treasury to satisfy those obligations. This report mostly discusses trends in outlays.

Budget Authority and Outlays

The distinction between outlays and BA is important to understanding the federal budget and, particularly, discretionary spending. Appropriations legislation controls discretionary funding and provides budget authority to fund specific programs. Congress exercises its constitutional power of the purse by deciding what funds federal agencies can obligate on behalf of the U.S. government, for what purposes and for specified time periods. While budget authority is available for just a single year (such as for most personnel compensation costs), some appropriations (such as for many military construction projects) provide budget authority for multiple years, or indefinitely.[3] Agencies obligate funds by signing contracts or hiring employees or contractors or in other ways. Budget authority has been compared to funds deposited into a checking account, which then can be used for specified federal purposes.

Outlays are disbursed federal funds. Outlays are recorded when the U.S. Treasury disburses appropriated funds to purchase goods and services, pay employees, issue benefits, or make interest payments. Agencies typically do not spend all of their budget authority in the year it becomes available, which implies that outlays will lag behind budget authority.

Outlay data are used to assess the macroeconomic effects of the federal budget, whereas budget analysis of specific federal programs is often based on budget authority, because that is what Congress controls directly. Limits on discretionary spending set by the Budget Control Act of 2011 (BCA; P.L. 112-25) and modified by subsequent acts are defined in terms of BA.

CATEGORIES OF FEDERAL SPENDING

Federal spending can be divided into three basic budget categories:

- discretionary spending ($1,226 billion in FY2013 outlays);
- mandatory spending ($2,094 billion in FY2013 outlays); and
- net interest costs ($215 billion in FY2013).[4]

Mandatory programs and net interest costs are the other components of federal spending.[5] Mandatory spending, also known as direct spending, funds entitlement programs, the Supplemental Nutrition Assistance Program (SNAP; formerly known as the Food Stamps program), and other spending controlled by laws other than appropriation acts.[6] Spending levels for mandatory programs generally depend on eligibility criteria, size of the eligible population, and participation rates.

Different types of mandatory programs are set up in diverse ways, reflecting historical influences, technical demands, and specific legislative authorities. While the term "entitlement" can be defined to coincide with the mandatory programs, many would distinguish programs providing benefits to large populations meeting set eligibility requirements from more special payments, such as salaries of judges covered by Article III of the Constitution.

In some cases, mandatory and discretionary spending support similar activities. For example, Medicare health care benefits are classified as mandatory spending, while most health care benefits for veterans and military personnel are classified as discretionary spending.

Legislative procedures for funding discretionary programs differ from those for mandatory programs.[7] Congress provides discretionary funds (BA) each year through the annual appropriations process. Other types of legislation, such as authorization measures, control mandatory spending. Some mandatory programs, such as Social Security, are financed outside the annual appropriations process. Other mandatory programs, such as Medicaid, are funded through appropriations measures, while the level of spending reflects eligibility requirements and other provisions set in authorizing legislation, as well as the pool of potential beneficiaries and program participation rates.[8]

Table 1 provides a simple division of federal spending (i.e., mandatory and discretionary spending) by contrasting the type of budget authority needed for specific purposes.

Table 1. Schematic Division of Budget Categories

	Budget Authority Provided by Law Other than Appropriation Acts	Budget Authority Provided by Appropriation Acts
Entitlement	Medicare Social Security	Appropriated entitlements (e.g., veterans' compensation, Medicaid, TANFa) SNAPb (with caveats)
Not an Entitlement	Salaries for Article III Judges Mandatory non-entitlements (e.g., Forest Service payments to states)	Discretionary spending (defense, non-defense discretionary; covers most costs of running agencies)

Source: Compiled by CRS.

[a] Temporary Assistance for Needy Families.

[b] The Supplemental Nutrition Assistance Program (SNAP) was formerly known as the Food Stamps program.

RECENT FISCAL POLICY AND DISCRETIONARY SPENDING

Policy disagreements about fiscal policy challenges continue to influence trends in discretionary spending. Fiscal policy describes how a government chooses to balance spending and revenues, which can be used to influence the level of economic activity.[9] Substantial evidence suggests that fiscal policy can stimulate economic activity when an economy is operating below its potential level of output and when short-term interest rates are near zero.[10]

Discretionary spending, which is controlled through an annual budget process, is potentially a more flexible fiscal instrument than mandatory spending. Some features of mandatory programs have often been changed to respond to economic conditions. For example, the period of eligibility for unemployment insurance benefits has often been changed during recessions.[11] Tax policy changes have also been used to respond to macroeconomic conditions. In addition, as incomes fall during recessions, tax revenues fall and more families become eligible for means-tested mandatory programs, deficits rise which helps dampen economic shocks.[12] When economic growth resumes, those changes run in the opposite direction. Those changes are therefore known as automatic stabilizers.

Fiscal Policy Complicated by Slow Recovery

Addressing short-term and long-term challenges simultaneously is difficult because additional government outlays, according to most economic research, would boost economic recovery, while reducing spending could help enhance fiscal sustainability—as would increases in federal revenues. Some have called for linking a package of policies to provide short-term fiscal stimulus with longer-term measures aimed at fiscal sustainability, although designing such packages to ensure credibility and effectiveness could be challenging.[13]

Financial Crisis and Recession

The 2007-2009 financial crisis and the recession that followed continue to color current fiscal policy debates. During the economic recession that followed the 2007-2009 financial crisis, the federal government took several measures to stimulate the economy, in addition to an extraordinary set of measures aimed at housing and credit markets. Some policymakers have called for expansion or continuation of programs intended to alleviate economic vulnerabilities of households and businesses, while other policymakers have argued that discretionary spending should revert to pre-crisis levels. Whether the federal government should take immediate steps to close the gap between spending and receipts or wait until the economy is more fully recovered has been subject to debate among economists.

While much of the funds made available by measures responding to the financial crisis or the subsequent recession were classified as mandatory or revenue reductions, discretionary spending also rose sharply. Most notably, Congress in early 2009 responded to weak economic conditions and dramatic job losses that sharply increased unemployment rates by passing a major fiscal stimulus package. The resulting measure, the American Recovery and Reinvestment Act of 2009 (ARRA; H.R. 1, P.L. 111-5), enacted on February 17, 2009, included stimulus spending and tax cuts estimated at the time to total $787.2 billion, including about $300 billion in discretionary spending.[14] ARRA included funds for discretionary spending on education initiatives, support for state governments, public housing, infrastructure, and health care.[15] In 2012, CBO estimated the total budgetary effect of ARRA at $831 billion between 2009 and 2019.[16]

The recovery after the deep recession that followed the 2007-2009 financial crisis has been relatively slow. Economic growth in the United States, however, has been faster in recent years than in many other advanced economies.[17] Economic recoveries following major financial crises can be much less robust than recoveries following more cyclical downturns.[18] Some continue to call for a more expansionary fiscal policy to respond to high unemployment levels, which would entail larger budget deficits in the short run.[19] Other economists are skeptical that such fiscal policies would ameliorate deeper problems caused by high personal and federal debt levels, and therefore call for fiscal restraint as a first step towards addressing longer-term fiscal challenges, or at least a transition to a less expansionary fiscal policy.[20] A 2012 International Monetary Fund (IMF) survey found that the experience of advanced countries during the recent recession suggests that active fiscal policy can stimulate economic growth when economic resources are not being fully used and when the effectiveness of standard monetary policy tools is constrained by very low interest rates.[21]

Faster Growth on the Horizon?

Most macroeconomic forecasters expect faster economic growth in 2014 than in 2013, although the recovery from the recent recession has been slower than most previous downturns.[22] Reductions in government spending are expected to dampen economic growth in the short run, although the recovery of key economic sectors such as housing are expected to strengthen.[23] Serious risks to economic recovery persist, such as those linked to the Eurozone and signs of decelerating growth in other countries such as China.[24]

DISCRETIONARY SPENDING LIMITS REIMPOSED IN 2011

Recent trends in discretionary spending have been controlled by statutory limits reestablished in the Budget Control Act of 2011 (BCA), enacted on August 2, 2011. Those limits, which originally extended until FY2021, are expected to shape future trends in discretionary spending. Subsequent legislation has modified those limits in ways discussed below.

Budget Control Act of 2011 (BCA)

Provisions of the BCA are projected to bring discretionary spending as a share of GDP to levels well below that seen in recent decades. In terms of real dollars (i.e., adjusting for inflation but not for growth in population or the economy), discretionary base defense spending was slated to revert to a level slightly above its FY2007 level, while non-defense discretionary spending was slated to revert a level near its 2002 level.[25]

The BCA set limits on discretionary spending that were initially estimated to save about $900 billion over the next decade relative to a pre-BCA baseline.[26] The BCA also established a Joint Select Committee on Deficit Reduction (JSC), known as the "Super Committee," to develop and present a plan to Congress and the President that would achieve an additional $1.2 trillion or more in savings. The BCA, in return, allowed a set of increases to the debt limit, subject to congressional disapproval, enabling the government to borrow through February 2013.[27] The BCA tied the expected reduction in spending achieved through those discretionary spending limits and other budget enforcement measures to increases in the debt limit of the same magnitude.[28]

FY2013 Sequestration Triggered

The Super Committee (JSC) reached a deadlock shortly before a key November 2011 deadline, thus triggering backup enforcement mechanisms set up in the BCA to reduce spending by $1.2 trillion. Those backup enforcement mechanisms have been modified by ATRA (more below). The original BCA caps were then superseded by *revised caps*, which imposed separate limits on defense (budget function 050) and non-defense spending. The sum of total discretionary spending under the original and revised caps was the same. Further reductions of $109 billion for each year from the revised cap levels, split between defense and non-defense, were slated to occur in each year from FY2013 through FY2021. Those reductions, along with interest savings, were designed to capture the $1.2 trillion in budget savings in the absence of a Super Committee plan.

For FY2013, the BCA had required a sequester on January 2, 2013—a cancellation of budget authority relying on pro-rata cuts to most discretionary budget authority, Medicare, and certain other mandatory outlays. Most mandatory spending was exempt from sequestration and Medicare patient care reductions are limited to 2%. Thus, the bulk of sequestration reductions applied to discretionary programs.

For later years—from FY2014 through FY2021—the BCA-specified mechanisms set *lowered spending caps* that would apply to discretionary funding levels. Within limits set by those caps, however, Congress would have flexibility to tailor the budget to suit its policy priorities. Amounts above those caps, according to budget law, would be subject to a cap enforcement sequester.[29]

A continuing resolution (CR; H.J.Res. 117; P.L. 112-175) was enacted on September 28, 2012, to fund the federal government for the first six months of the fiscal year.[30] In general, funding levels were set 0.612% above FY2012 levels, with exceptions for war funding and certain disaster relief programs.[31] Discretionary spending in the CR was scored at $1,047 billion, which equaled the sum of the revised defense and non-defense caps. Base budget discretionary defense funding, however, was scored at $557 billion (in BA), or $11 billion above the revised BCA cap, while nondefense discretionary spending (BA) was scored at $490 billion, or $11 billion below its BCA revised cap.[32] Funding in the CR above cap levels would have been subject to a cap enforcement sequester, absent subsequent changes.[33] The American Taxpayer Relief Act (see below) delayed both the Super Committee sequester and the potential cap enforcement sequester, in addition to other changes in budget enforcement mechanisms.

Scaling Down Sequestration and the Fiscal Cliff

The American Taxpayer Relief Act (ATRA; H.R. 8; P.L. 112-240) delayed the sequester triggered by the absence of a Super Committee (JSC) plan by two months, from January 2, 2013 to March 1, 2013.[34] In addition, the size of those FY2013 sequestration cuts was reduced from $109 billion to $85 billion.[35] The remaining $85 billion sequester, as before, was divided equally between defense and non-defense spending. Nearly all of the sequester reductions in defense spending fell within discretionary spending, while about a third of non-defense sequester reductions fell within the mandatory category.

Half of the $24 billion reduction in the size of the FY2013 sequester was offset by lowering discretionary spending limits for FY2013 by $4 billion ($2 billion in security spending; $2 billion in non-security spending) and lowering limits for FY2014 by $8 billion ($4 billion in defense; $4 billion in non-defense). The remaining $12 billion was offset by revenue changes affecting retirement accounts.[36]

ATRA also altered discretionary spending limits on FY2013 discretionary spending. ATRA delayed a potential cap enforcement sequester to enforce discretionary spending limits from early January 2013 to March 27, 2013.[37] The cap enforcement sequester was modified by ATRA to apply to security/non-security categories, rather than the defense/non-defense categories previously in effect.[38] Because the full-year funding measure (H.R. 933; P.L. 113-6) was designed to conform to these modified discretionary spending limits, the cap sequester was avoided.[39]

The discretionary spending limits enforced by that sequester, however, effectively set top-line totals for the FY2013 full-year funding measure.

The change in the FY2013 discretionary limits from defense/non-defense to security/non-security may have shifted the allocation of spending reductions. Because the security category is broader than the defense category, cap enforcement sequester reductions would have applied to a larger pool of programs.

The cap enforcement sequester would have reduced spending within security programs by more than within non-security programs because the CR funded defense programs above BCA cap levels. Without changes in spending levels, the cap enforcement sequester, according to CBO estimates, would have reduced security spending by $7 billion and non-security spending by $1 billion.[40]

ATRA also put in place a less restrictive fiscal policy by extending various expiring tax provisions and extended unemployment benefits, while postponing across-the-board sequestration until March 2013.[41] Those increases in federal revenues and decreases in spending, often known as the "fiscal cliff," would have lowered the federal deficit dramatically, but could have led to a new recession in 2013, according to CBO and other forecasters.[42]

Others, however, had expected more modest macroeconomic consequences from those changes.[43]

Attempts to Avoid the Effects of Sequestration

Many have objected to the consequences for federal programs and fiscal policy of the BCA's sequestration measures. Various proposals to delay, replace, or modify sequestration have been put forth. The potential effects of defense and non-defense cuts have also been discussed in various committee hearings.[44] The Reducing Flight Delays Act of 2013 (P.L. 113-9), enacted May 1, 2013, authorized the Secretary of Transportation to transfer funds to Federal Aviation Administration (FAA) appropriations accounts in order to reduce delays due to furloughs of FAA personnel.

Congressional Initiatives

The House-passed FY2013 budget resolution (H.Con.Res. 112; agreed to on March 29, 2012, on a 228-191 vote) called for the cancellation of the January 2013 sequester, conditional on achieving savings in domestic programs through reconciliation procedures.[45] Such reconciliation procedures, however, would only come into play with the agreement of the Senate. On May 10, 2012, the House took another step to modify sequestration by passing the Sequester Replacement Reconciliation Act of 2012 (H.R. 5652; 218-199, 1 present). The measure, according to CBO's analysis, would limit the effect of sequestration by an estimated $72.2 billion over the next 10 years, largely by protecting defense unobligated balances and certain non-defense advance appropriations.[46] The measure would also reduce the cap on FY2013 discretionary spending by $19 billion, from its current level of $1,047 billion.

On December 19, House Majority Whip Eric Cantor introduced H.R. 6684, the Spending Reduction Act of 2012. That measure resembles H.R. 5652, except that a flood insurance title, which had been enacted separately, was omitted. In addition, certain effective dates were also changed.[47] In the 113th Congress, Representative Ellison introduced one bill to avoid sequestration (H.R. 505) and Senator Whitehouse introduced two measures to replace the Budget Control Act (S. 277 and S. 278).

On the day before that sequester was issued, Congress considered other measures that would have modified or replaced it. The Senate considered S. 16, a sequester replacement bill introduced by Senator Inhofe, and S. 388, introduced by Senator Mikulski. Neither measure was passed. The budget resolution measure reported by the Senate Budget Committee (S.Con.Res. 8) on March 14, 2013, proposed replacing sequestration reduction with a mix of other spending reductions and revenue increases.

On February 27, 2013, Senator James Inhofe introduced S. 16, a bill that proposed that the President submit a sequester replacement plan to Congress by March 15, 2013. The plan would be subject to a joint resolution of disapproval that would be considered under expedited procedures. A motion to proceed to consideration of S. 16 was withdrawn on February 28, 2013, following an unsuccessful motion on cloture (38-62).

On April 23, 2013, Majority Leader Harry Reid introduced S. 788, which would cancel the discretionary portion of the FY2013 BCA sequester (see next section) as well as some of the across-the-board reductions included in the full-year FY2013 funding measure (H.R. 933; P.L. 113-6; discussed below).[48] The bill would also change how BCA discretionary spending caps would be adjusted for war funding (OCO/GWOT). Under current law, BCA caps are adjusted upwards by the amount of OCO funds (and for other items such as certain program integrity and disaster costs). The proposed legislation would limit the OCO adjustment to the BCA security cap to the amount of current OCO funding proposed by the Administration, or the actual amount of OCO appropriations if that were less than those proposed levels.[49] The difference between those proposed OCO cap levels and baseline spending projections would total nearly $135 billion for FY2014-FY2016.

Numerous other measures to replace or modify the BCA sequester were also introduced in both the 112th and 113th Congresses.

Administration Proposals to Modify BCA Caps

The President's FY2013 budget request essentially conformed to the original BCA caps, but argues that the January 2013 sequester and other backup enforcement measures should be cancelled because Administration proposals would achieve savings in other ways. In February 2013, President Obama called for avoiding sequestration by substituting tax increases and targeted spending cuts.[50]

BCA Sequester Issued March 1, 2013

On March 1, 2013, the President signed a sequester order that cancelled $85 billion in budgetary resources, a measure triggered by the absence of a JSC ("Super Committee") plan to reduce the federal deficit.[51] Reductions were split equally between defense and non-defense categories.

Nearly all the defense reductions were taken in discretionary programs because less than $1 billion in defense mandatory spending was sequestrable.[52]

The President chose to exempt Military Personnel accounts from sequestration, which required larger reductions in other defense accounts. Non-exempt defense discretionary accounts were reduced by 7.8% for a total reduction of $42.6 billion in budgetary resources. While war (Overseas Contingency Operations; OCO) funding was not subject to BCA caps, it was not exempted from sequestration. Former Defense Secretary Leon Panetta, however, indicated that the Defense Department would take steps to protect funding for war operations by finding other cuts.[53] In addition, unobligated balances in defense accounts were also sequestered.

The sequester reduced non-defense discretionary program funding by 5.0%, which reflected a $25.8 billion reduction in budgetary resources.[54] The remainder of non-defense reductions ($16.9 billion) was absorbed by non-defense mandatory programs. A 2% reduction in Medicare patient care accounted for most of the non-defense mandatory savings ($11.3 billion), while a 5.1% sequester was applied to other non-exempt mandatory programs, yielding another $5.5 billion in budgetary savings.

The Super Committee sequester reduced federal outlays in FY2013 by considerably less than the total reduction applied to budgetary resources. This reflects the usual lag between reductions in budget authority and reductions in obligations and outlays, as well as the time agencies require to implement plans to reduce their spending. In addition, special budgetary rules delay the start of the sequester of Medicare patient care outlays by a month.[55] CBO has estimated that the BCA sequester would reduce FY2013 outlays by $42 billion in FY2013.[56]

Full-Year Funding for FY2013

On March 6, 2013, the House passed a measure (H.R. 933) to fund the government for the remainder of FY2013 by a 267-151 vote. The measure provided detailed appropriations levels for Defense and Military Construction-Veterans' programs. Other programs, with some exceptions, were funded near FY2012 levels before taking into account a series of across-the-board reductions.[57] Spending reductions in the bill would not have affected the amount of reductions in spending made through the March 1, 2013 (JSC/Super Committee) sequester.[58]

On March 11, 2013, a substitute measure for H.R. 933 was posted on the Senate Committee on Appropriations website. According to Senate Appropriations Chair Barbara Mikulski, defense and military construction-veterans provisions of the substitute measure matched those in the House-passed H.R. 933.[59] The measure would have provided more detailed spending adjustments in other areas.

Both H.R. 933 and the Senate alternative were scored as conforming with discretionary spending caps as revised by ATRA (totaling $1,043 billion for regular appropriations) and thus avoided a cap enforcement sequester.[60] That scored total did not include war funding, emergency-designated spending, and program integrity funding.

The Senate passed an amended version of H.R. 933 by a 73-26 vote on March 20, 2013. The Senate version of H.R. 933 included detailed changes in spending levels for programs within the Agriculture, Commerce-Justice-Science, and Homeland Security areas, in addition to the changes in Defense, Military Construction-Veterans that the House measure had included. Most other programs received funding close to FY2012 levels. The House agreed to Senate changes the next day on a 318-109 vote. While some of the effects of sequestration were adjusted by reallocating spending reductions, the amount of the March 1 sequester cuts remained in place. The President signed the measure (P.L. 113-6) on March 26, 2013.

Discretionary Funding for FY2014

Submission of the Obama Administration's FY2014 budget was delayed until April 10, 2013, due to substantial changes enacted by ATRA at the beginning of January 2013 and the demands of the March 1, 2013, JSC sequester. The President's FY2014 budget request proposed several modifications of BCA caps on discretionary spending. The Administration proposed that FY2014 spending limits be set at revised cap levels (i.e., $552 billion for defense and $506 billion for nondefense) rather than lowered cap levels (i.e., $498.1 billion for defense and $469.4 billion for non-defense), which would have allowed higher levels of discretionary spending while the economy is recovering from a major recession. Spending limits for the second half of the FY2013-FY2021 budget window, in the Administration's proposals, would have been lowered by $60 billion each for defense and non-defense. In addition, discretionary caps would have been extended to FY2022 and FY2023.

The Administration estimated that those spending cap modifications would reduce discretionary spending by $202 billion over FY2014-FY2023.[61] Thus, projected discretionary spending for FY2014-FY2018 shown in the figures below, which presume the President's budgetary proposals are adopted, reflects an assumption that BCA constraints on discretionary spending would be loosened in FY2014 and tightened later, starting in FY2017. The Administration's FY2014 budget plan also includes $260 billion in unspecified reductions in discretionary spending, mostly slated for FY2015 through FY2023.[62] If those reductions were carried out, discretionary spending levels would have been less than those shown in figures below.

During the FY2014 budget cycle, the House and Senate responded to the budgetary challenges presented by BCA caps in different ways. Just before the August 2013 recess, the gap between House and Senate totals for FY2014 discretionary spending stood at about $90 billion. The House Appropriations Committee set suballocations for its subcommittees that totaled $973.1 billion, slightly above total discretionary spending at BCA lowered caps levels ($967.5 billion) for FY2014.[63] Senate Appropriations Committee guidance for its subcommittees, however, indicated a total for FY2014 consistent with BCA revised caps (i.e., a total of $1,058 billion split between a base defense subtotal of $552 billion and a non-defense total of $506 billion).[64]

Differences between House and Senate discretionary spending levels were not resolved before the start of FY2014 on October 1, 2013, which resulted in a shutdown of most federal operations.[65] Funding for federal operations was restored by passage of a continuing resolution (H.R. 2775) on October 16, 2013, which was signed by the President the following morning (Continuing Appropriations Act, 2014; P.L. 113-46). The measure provides funding on an annualized basis of $986.3 billion before adjustments.[66]

The Bipartisan Budget Act of 2013

The Bipartisan Budget Act of 2013 (BBA; H.J.Res. 59; P.L. 113-67) provided a reconciliation of House and Senate discretionary spending levels for the remainder of FY2014 and for FY2015 as well. Final House approval was obtained on a 332-94 vote on December 12, 2013, and the Senate approved the final version on December 18, 2013, on a 64-36 vote.

The BBA set discretionary defense spending caps at $520.464 billion for FY2014 and $521.272 billion for FY2015. Non-defense caps were set at $491.773 billion for FY2014 and $492.356 billion for FY2015.[67] The mechanism for reducing the revised BCA caps to lowered caps levels in order to capture savings not attained by the Joint Select Committee on Deficit Reduction (JSC) was turned off for both FY2014 and FY2015.[68] Both modified defense and nondefense spending limits for FY2014 were $22.4 billion above the lowered caps levels that would have applied in the absence of the Bipartisan Budget Act, while FY2015 levels were about $9 billion higher.[69]

Final Appropriations for FY2014

The House and Senate Appropriations Committees announced an agreement on funding for the remainder of FY2014 on January 13, 2014. The resulting measure (Senate Amendment to H.R. 3547) was scored as conforming to caps set in the Bipartisan Budget Act of 2014.[70] The House voted to accept the measure on January 14, 2014, on a 359-67 vote. On the following day, the Senate approved that version on a 72-26 vote. The President then signed the measure (P.L. 113- 76) on January 17, 2014.

A short-term continuing resolution (H.J.Res. 106) was introduced by House Appropriations Chairman Harold Rogers to extend federal funding from January 15 to January 18, 2014, to provide more time for the consideration of final FY2014 appropriations. On January 14, 2014, that measure passed the House on a voice vote and the Senate on an 86-14 vote. The President signed the measure (P.L. 113-73) on the following day.

Table 2 summarizes discretionary funding and modifications of statutory caps on discretionary funding for base defense and nondefense funding from for the period FY2013 through FY2021. Levels are shown in terms of scored budget authority (BA) that excludes war (Overseas Contingency Operations/OCO), disaster, program integrity, and emergency funding. The first two rows in both the defense and nondefense categories show revised caps before and after the fiscal cliff agreement (ATRA), which reduced the size of the JSC sequester. The next pair of rows show estimates of post-sequester funding in FY2013 and OMB estimates of lowered cap levels in subsequent years. Next, the modifications of the defense and non-defense caps enacted in December 2013 by the Bipartisan Budget Act are shown. That act turned off the mechanism that lowers caps to recapture savings not obtained by the JSC for FY2014 and FY2015, but did not change caps or the cap-lowering mechanism for later years. Finally, a pre-BCA Administration projection (CBO reestimate of the FY2012 plan) and the totals for the FY2014 budget submission are presented.

Preview of FY2015 Appropriations

The Bipartisan Budget Act (P.L. 113-67; sections 115 and 116) provides authority for budgetary enforcement "in the same manner as for a concurrent resolution on the budget for FY2015" if no budget resolution were agreed to by the House and Senate by April 15, 2014. In each chamber, the chairman of the Budget Committee would then be mandated to submit information normally contained in a budget resolution after April 15 but before May 15, 2014.

The President's budget submission is due by the first Monday in February, although no sanctions attach to late submissions.[71] An OMB spokesman stated that the FY2015 budget proposal would be submitted on March 4, 2014.[72] Some attribute the delay in the budget submission to the delayed completion of FY2014 appropriations, which then pushed back budget formulation deadlines.[73] The FY2014 budget, as noted above, was submitted on April 10, 2013. OMB instructed federal agencies to submit plans that would reflect a 5% reduction in net discretionary funding, along with measures to reach a 10% reduction in net discretionary funding.[74] Treasury Secretary Jacob Lew stated that the upcoming budget would reflect a "balanced approach to having long-term fiscal policies."[75]

The Congressional Budget Office stated that its budget outlook, which will contain updated economic and budgetary baseline projections through FY2024, will be released on February 4, 2014.[76]

LONG-TERM TRENDS IN DISCRETIONARY SPENDING

Discretionary Spending Now a Smaller Share of Federal Spending

The composition of the federal budget has changed dramatically since the early 1960s. As **Figure 1** shows, discretionary spending as a share of the federal budget has fallen, while mandatory spending's share has steadily increased.[77] Discretionary spending will thus have gone from comprising two-thirds of federal spending in FY1962 to only 35% of total outlays in 2013.[78] That share is expected to decline further to 24% in FY2023, according to CBO baseline projections.[79]

Table 2. Defense and Nondefense Trends Under Revised BCA Constraints

Budget Authority in Billions of Dollars; Excludes OCO/War, Disaster, Program Integrity, and Emergency Funding

Defense (base)	FY2013	FY2014	FY2015	FY2016	FY2017	FY2018	FY2019	FY2020	FY2021
BCA revised cap									
Pre-fiscal cliff deal (ATRA)	546	556	566	577	590	603	616	630	644
Post-fiscal cliff deal (ATRA)*	544	552	← unchanged →						
Sequester/OMB Seq. Preview Reports									
JSC Sequester/Auto Enforcement†	-42.6	-53.9	-54.0	-54	-54	-54	-54	-54	-54
Sequester/Lowered Caps*	517.9	498.1	512	523	536	549	562	576	590
BBA 2013 caps		520.5	521.3		← unchanged: same as pre-ATRA revised caps →				
FY2014 final base defense funding scored as meeting FY2014 BBA cap		Caps not to be lowered			Subject to lowering of caps				
Administration Plans									
Pre BCA: FY2012 Plan, (CBO reestimate, March 2011)	596	612	624	637	649	661	673	685	697
Most recent: FY2014 Plan (OMB April 2013)		552	566	577	586	595	604	614	624

Non-Defense	FY2013	FY2014	FY2015	FY2016	FY2017	FY2018	FY2019	FY2020	FY2021
BCA revised cap									
Pre-fiscal cliff deal (ATRA)	501	510	520	530	541	553	566	578	590
Post-fiscal cliff deal (ATRA)*	499	506	← unchanged →						
Sequester/OMB Seq. Preview Reports									
JSC Sequester/Auto Enforcement†	-25.8	-36.6	0	0	0	0	0	0	0
Sequester/Lowered Caps*‡	470	469.4	520.0	530	541	553	566	578	590
BBA 2013 caps		491.8	492.4	← unchanged: same as pre-ATRA revised caps →					
FY2014 final base nondefense funding scored as meeting FY2014 BBA cap		Caps not to be lowered		Subject to lowering of caps					
Administration Plans									
Pre BCA: FY2012 Plan, (CBO reestimate, March 2011)	550	550	559	573	586	601	617	638	646
Most recent: FY2014 Plan (OMB April 2013)	503	506	536	545	556	568	581	599	603
Unspecified reductions**			-16	-15	-19	-23	-27	-37	-33

Table 2. (Continued)

	FY2013	FY2014	FY2015	FY2016	FY2017	FY2018	FY2019	FY2020	FY2021
Non-Defense									
Net (see OMB Table S-10 nondefense category)		506	520	530	537	545	554	562	570

Source: CRS calculations based on the following data sources: OMB Sequestration Report, March 1, 2013; OMB Sequestration Preview Report for FY2014 (Corrected version); CBO, Reestimate of the President's Budget, March 2011; CBO, "2014 Discretionary Appropriations Including H.R. 3547, as Posted on House Rules Website on January 13, Excluding OCO, Disaster, Prog. Int. and Emergencies," January 14, 2014. CBO, "Estimate of Discretionary Budget Authority for Fiscal Year 2013, Showing Amounts for Defense and Nondefense Programs," September 10, 2013, available at http://www.cbo.gov/sites/default/files/cbofiles /attachments/09-10-2013- Supplement%20_to_Table3_from_May_Outlook.xls; OMB, *FY2014 Mid-Session Review*, Tables S-9 and S-10, available at http://www.whitehouse.gov/sites/default/files/omb/ budget/fy2014/assets/14msr.pdf;OMB, FY2014 Analytical Perspectives, Table 31-1, "Policy Budget Authority and Outlay by Function, Category, and Program." H.Rept. 113-290 (to accompany H.Res. 438).

Notes: CBO describes lowered caps as "Caps established by the Budget Control Act, including automatic spending reductions." Above caps are "scored" numbers, which will generally differ from non-scored budget totals. FY2013 caps revised as part of fiscal cliff deal, caps applied to security/nonsecurity basis. Defense and nondefense post-ATRA caps were in effect used to calculate JSC sequester.

* ATRA redefined FY2013 discretionary spending caps using categories of "security" and "non-security," which served to bind discretionary spending levels. Defense and non-defense categories were used to calculate the March 1, 2013 sequestration, but did not bind discretionary spending levels.

† The JSC sequester/automatic enforcement discretionary spending reduction will not equal the difference between the revised cap and sequester/lowered cap level because (i) for FY2013 the defense/non-defense cap was not binding; and (ii) some spending not covered by the defense/non-defense cap is subject to sequestration. For example, war funding (OCO) is not covered by the defense cap, but is subject to sequestration under section 251A of the BBEDCA. More precisely, caps are adjusted upwards to

accommodate funding for war funding (OCO) and emergency items, and within specified limits, to accommodate funding for disaster relief and program integrity initiatives.

** According to the FY2014 *Mid-Session Review*, "The 2014 Budget includes allowances, similar to the Function 920 allowances used in Budget Resolutions, to represent amounts to be allocated among the respective agencies to reach the proposed defense and non-defense caps for 2015 and beyond. These levels are determined for illustrative purposes but do not reflect specific policy decisions." See fn. 5, to MSR Table S-10, p. 58.

FY2014 OMB net nondefense discretionary proposal levels do not reflect proposed reclassifications between mandatory and discretionary categories. Unspecified reductions for subfunctions 053 and 054 total $5.4 billion over FY2014-FY2023 and do not exceed $1 billion until FY2022. For the sake of compactness, those reductions are not shown. Unspecified subfunction 051 and 053 reductions reported in OMB, FY2014 *Analytical Perspectives*, Table 31-1. No unspecified reductions are proposed for subfunction 051 (Defense-Military).

‡ CBO estimated FY2013 nondefense spending at $483.6 billion in September 2013. That estimate excluded an $18.6 billion offset for changes in mandatory spending (CHIMPs) and did not reflect a $5 billion increase in estimated Federal Housing Administration receipts due to higher mortgage insurance charges. The FY2013 estimate of $470 billion includes those adjustments.

Mandatory spending, by contrast, has risen from 26% of total outlays in FY1962 to 59% in 2013. Net interest accounted for 6% of federal outlays in FY1962 and in FY2012. Net interest costs, according to CBO baseline projections, are expected to rise sharply to 14% in FY2023 as interest rates return to more normal levels and the federal debt continues to expand.

Discretionary Spending As a Share of GDP

Trends in discretionary spending as a share of gross domestic product (GDP) provide another perspective on how the composition of federal outlays has changed. Measuring budget components as a share of GDP compares their size to the economy as a whole, and implicitly incorporates inflation and population growth. When GDP falls, however, the percentage of outlays to GDP tends to rise. **Figure 2** shows components of federal spending as a percentage of GDP since 1962.

Total federal outlays as a share of GDP peaked in 2009 as a result of the current economic situation and federal interventions. While discretionary outlays declined as a percentage of total outlays in 2009, they rose as a percentage of GDP because the economy shrank in 2008 and early 2009. Since 2010, discretionary outlays have been falling, both in current dollar terms and as a percentage of GDP. If caps on discretionary spending remain in place, discretionary spending will continue to fall as a share of GDP. In May 2013, CBO projected that under current law discretionary spending would fall to 5.5% of GDP by FY2023. That share would be about 15% lower than its minimum share during the 1990s (6.2% in FY1999).

Because of the decline in discretionary spending as a percentage of total outlays and as a percentage of GDP and the resulting increase in the share of mandatory spending over time, controlling the federal budget may have become more difficult for Congress. Roughly speaking, discretionary defense and discretionary non-defense outlays each comprise about one-seventh of the federal budget.

In other words, because net interest payments and mandatory spending are set automatically, less money is available to allocate to other government agencies and programs unless revenues rise or Congress modifies eligibility requirements and benefits of mandatory spending programs.

Because discretionary funding is provided through an annual budgeting process, this may have made it easier to target spending restrictions on discretionary programs.

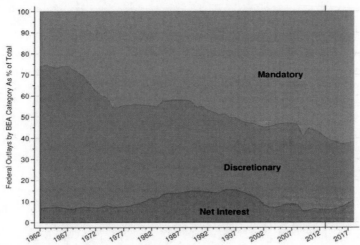

Source: CRS calculations based on OMB FY2014 data.

Notes: FY2012 values estimated; FY2013-FY2018 values reflect President's budget
   proposals.

Figure 1. Outlays by Category as a Percentage of Total Outlays; FY1962-FY2018.

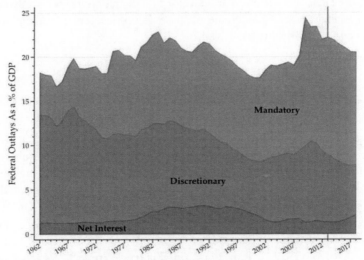

Source: CRS calculations based on OMB FY2013 data.

Notes: FY2013 values estimated; FY2013-FY2018 values reflect President's budget
   proposals and OMB GDP projections.

Figure 2. Components of Federal Spending, FY1962-FY2018; FY1962-FY2018.

Most large mandatory programs are linked to people's retirement decisions, so abrupt changes in benefit levels or eligibility criteria could disrupt financial plans of those already retired or about to retire.[80] In the past, mandatory programs such as Social Security and Medicare have enjoyed broad bipartisan support. Those considerations may complicate efforts to reduce funding for mandatory programs.

Costs linked to the retirement of the baby-boom generation, born in the years following World War II, are a major cause of rising mandatory spending. As the U.S. population has aged, the composition of federal outlays has evolved to reflect needs of the elderly.

On the other hand, the current trajectory of federal spending on health care appears unsustainable, and could place heavy fiscal burdens on younger generations and generations not yet born.[81]

DISCRETIONARY SPENDING AND NATIONAL PRIORITIES

Discretionary spending can be categorized in several different ways. These divisions provide a rough indicator of national priorities as reflected in federal spending decisions. Some of these categories play or have played a role in budget enforcement mechanisms.

Defense and Non-Defense Spending

One basic division of discretionary spending separates defense programs (budget function 050) from non-defense programs (everything else). Discretionary spending caps now in place due to the Budget Control Act, as modified, set separate limits for base budget defense funding and nondefense funding. Defense spending is typically divided between base budget and war spending, which supports activities within Overseas Contingency Operations (OCO) or Global War on Terror (GWOT).[82] **Figure 3** shows trends in discretionary defense and non-defense BA in real (i.e., inflation-adjusted) terms since FY1977.[83] Projections in **Figure 3** reflect spending paths conforming to the original BCA caps. As noted above, ATRA and the Bipartisan Budget Act of 2014 reduced the scope of BCA spending constraints for FY2013 and FY2014.

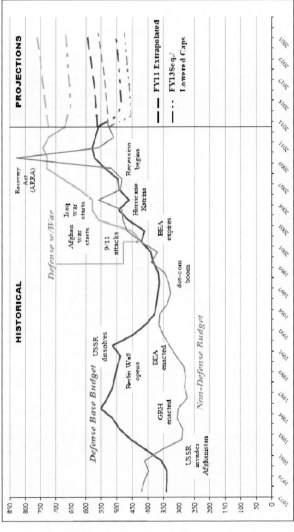

Source: CRS calculations based on CBO and OMB FY2013 historical budget data. See "An Update to the Budget and Economic Outlook: FY2012 to FY2022, August 2012, available at http://www.cbo.gov/sites/default/files/cbofiles/attachments/43539-08-22-2012-Update One-Col.pdf. OMB data are available at http://www.whitehouse.gov/omb/budget/Supplemental/. Estimates of war costs taken from CRS Report RL33110, *The Cost of Iraq, Afghanistan, and Other Global War on Terror Operations Since 9/11*, by Amy Belasco. Figure does not reflect changes in ATRA or the Sandy supplemental (P.L. 113-2).

Figure 3. Defense and Non-Defense Discretionary Spending, FY1977-FY2021; In Billions of FY2012 Dollars of Budget Authority.

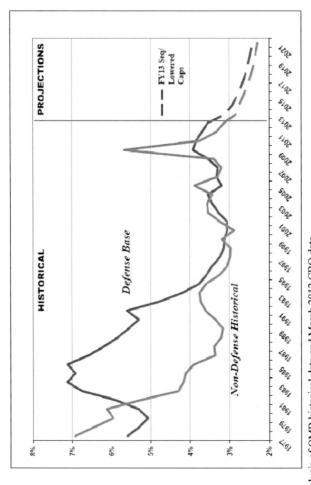

Source: CRS analysis of OMB historical data and March 2012 CBO data.

Notes: Defense is base discretionary funding within function 050; all other budget functions are defined as nondefense discretionary spending. FY2013-FY2021 reflect January 2013 sequester and later lowered caps. Estimates of war costs, which were subtracted, are taken from CRS Report RL33110, *The Cost of Iraq, Afghanistan, and Other Global War on Terror Operations Since 9/11*, by Amy Belasco.

Figure 4. Discretionary Budget Authority as % of GDP; FY1977-FY2021.

Spending trends can also be measured as shares of GDP, which reflects how federal spending compares with the size of the economy. **Figure 4** shows trends in base defense and non-defense discretionary BA as a share of GDP over the period 1969-2017. BA as a percentage of GDP reflects changes in population and growth in per-capita income, which may affect the costs of federal programs. How population changes affect federal spending may also depend on whether specific governmental services are subject to scale economies. For instance, a 10% increase in population might require resources devoted to individual health care services to rise by 10% in order to maintain the same level of service, other things equal. For many governmental services, one might expect to find substantial scale economies. For example, an increase in population would likely not be expected to raise the costs of information-generating activities, such as medical and scientific research, or national defense activities.

The Reagan Administration when it took office in 1981 sought to increase defense spending and reduce spending on domestic programs.[84] Budget enforcement measures were introduced in the mid-1980s to control rising federal deficits. In 1985, the Gramm-Rudman-Hollings (GRH) deficit control legislation and subsequent measures were enacted with the aim of constraining federal spending. In 1990, the Budget Enforcement Act (BEA; P.L. 101-508) set statutory caps on discretionary spending and imposed other budgetary enforcement mechanisms, which many analysts view as having helped constrain federal spending, increase federal revenues, and thus, reduce deficits. In the decade after the attacks of September 11, 2001 and the expiration of statutory spending caps at the end of FY2002, however, both defense and non-defense discretionary spending rose in real terms. Trends in defense and non-defense spending are discussed in more detail below.

Discretionary Defense Spending

Base budget defense spending in real terms has risen and fallen to reflect national security challenges and changes in policy priorities.[85] Defense spending increased sharply in the mid-1960s as the United States' involvement in Vietnam deepened. After large-scale withdrawals of American troops from Vietnam began in 1969, defense spending as a share of GDP fell for the next decade. In the mid-1970s, when the United States took a less confrontational diplomatic stance towards the Soviet Union, termed détente, defense spending grew modestly. The Soviet invasion of Afghanistan in 1979, however, prompted the Carter Administration, and then the Reagan Administration during the early 1980s to boost military expenditures. By the mid-1980s, however, concerns about large deficits helped constrain defense spending. After the fall of most European communist regimes in 1989 and the dissolution of the Soviet Union in 1991, defense spending declined. Costs of the first Iraq War (1990-1991) were shouldered by U.S. coalition partners.[86]

After the attacks of September 11, 2001, defense spending rose sharply as the United States began military operations in Afghanistan, but also included dramatic increases in non-war or base budget funding. War in Iraq, which began in 2003, amplified demands for higher defense spending. War costs have fallen since the drawdown of troops participating in the 2007 surge of forces in Iraq and the withdrawal of combat troops from Iraq at the end of calendar 2011. Further reductions in war costs are expected as troops are withdrawn from Afghanistan.[87] Decisions about major procurement programs and possible changes in Budget Control Act budget enforcement mechanisms could also affect trends in defense spending.

Ups and downs in defense spending have primarily reflected changes in investment funding for modernization of weapon systems and support equipment, and conducting Research, Development, Test & Evaluation (RDT&E) on new systems.[88] Defense investment typically grows when support for defense spending is high, such as in wartime or the early 1980s, and then falls as support dips and other issues become more pressing, with peaks in investment offsetting later valleys. Trends in base defense spending over the past decade may not reflect the full extent of the growth in defense costs, because it does not include about $300 billion in war-related investment in weapon systems, which will likely remain in the inventory for many years to come. By contrast, wartime operating costs, such as training and support of personnel, do not contribute to modernization.

Defense Spending As a Percentage of GDP

Discretionary defense spending accounts for a much smaller share of GDP in recent years than during World War II, the Korean War, or the Vietnam War.[89] At the height of the Vietnam War in FY1969, defense outlays were 8.7% of GDP. Moreover, with compulsory military service, which was in effect until 1973, the budgetary costs of war understated the full economic costs of national defense, because many draftees were prevented from pursuing other opportunities.[90]

As noted above, defense spending fell during the 1970s, rose rapidly following the Soviet invasion of Afghanistan, and fell after the collapse of most of the USSR's Warsaw Pact allied governments in 1989 and the dissolution of the USSR itself in 1991. Discretionary defense outlays, which had fallen to 3.0% of GDP by the late 1990s, rose sharply to 4.0% of GDP in 2005, and reached 4.7% of GDP in 2011, divided between 3.6% for the base defense budget and 1.1% for war funding (Overseas Contingency Operations; OCO). In FY2012 and FY2013 defense outlays as a share of GDP have been falling, in large part due to the withdrawal of combat troops from Iraq that was completed in December 2011. A withdrawal of most troops from Afghanistan is expected by the end of 2014.[91]

Increased defense outlays accounted for 53% of the real increase in total discretionary outlays over the decade of 2000-2010, rising 6.8% per year on average in real terms.[92]

How Much Defense Spending Is Appropriate?

The appropriate size of the defense budget has long been a lively topic of debate. In 2007, General Mike Mullen, then chairman of the Joint Chiefs of Staff, said that he considered 4% of GDP "an absolute floor" for future defense spending.[93] Some analysts have expressed some doubts about the sustainability of current defense budget plans.[94] Others contend that defense expenditures as a proportion of GDP should fall over the long term because the cost of defending the nation depends on factors that are largely independent of economic growth. Geopolitical challenges, wars, major procurement programs, and changes in national spending priorities have spurred swings in defense spending in past decades.

Former Secretary of Defense Robert Gates called for cost-cutting measures within the Department of Defense (DOD), although the stated aim is not to reduce the Department's top-line budget number.[95] Former Secretary of Defense Leon Panetta has raised concerns that cuts required by the Budget Control Act could have serious effects.[96] On the other hand, the Budget Control Act would have brought discretionary base defense spending in inflation-adjusted terms back to its FY2007 level. With modifications made in the American Taxpayer Relief Act of 2012 (see above), real discretionary base defense spending after sequestration would revert to a level between its FY2007 and FY2008 levels.

In early 2013, DOD leaders issued guidance on budget strategies to handle uncertainties raised by sequestration and the FY2013 continuing resolution (P.L. 112-175) that provides funding through March 27.[97] DOD budget guidance includes protection of war operations and programs associated with new strategic priorities; reduction of administrative and civilian personnel costs; and deferring less critical maintenance. Some analysts argue that budgetary constraints may require a larger reconsideration of strategic goals of DOD.[98]

Non-Defense Discretionary Spending

Non-defense spending supports the largest number of federal agencies and programs, including science and technology research, natural resources, energy, education, and numerous others. None of the individual programs within the non-defense discretionary category have approached 1% of GDP since 1962, and funding for most of these programs was less than 0.5% of GDP during that period.

Non-defense discretionary spending in recent decades has typically ranged between 3% and 4% of GDP. In 1969, during the Vietnam War, non-defense spending was 3.6% of GDP. After rising to a peak of 5.2% in 1980, non-defense discretionary spending's share of GDP fell during the Reagan Administration, reaching 3.5% of GDP in 1987.[99] Since then it fluctuated between 3.2% and 3.8% of GDP until 2009. Non-defense discretionary spending rose to 4.6% of GDP in 2010 reflecting a decline in GDP (reducing the denominator of that share) due to the economic recession and policy responses such as the American Recovery and Reinvestment Act of 2009 (ARRA; H.R. 1, P.L. 111-5). Since that year, non-defense discretionary spending has declined in real terms and as a percentage of GDP. According to CBO current-law projections, non-defense discretionary spending will fall to 2.7% in 2023.[100]

International Discretionary Spending

Some discretionary spending constraints in the 1980s and 1990s set separate caps for defense, domestic, and international (budget function 150) spending.[101] Demands for funding international programs have varied dramatically with changing geopolitical conditions.

In the past decade, international spending (budget function 150) has been strongly affected by wars in Afghanistan and Iraq. Discretionary spending for international programs since 1969 has averaged 0.3% of GDP, reaching its peak of 0.5% of GDP in 1975. International spending had trended downward from the early 1980s until the start of the Iraq war in 2003. Between 2001 and 2010, spending on international programs rose from 0.2% of GDP to 0.3% of GDP. The majority of the funding in this category in recent times has been devoted to diplomatic missions, foreign aid, and international finance. The future trajectory of international funding may depend on how the role of the United States evolves in Iraq, Afghanistan, and neighboring countries.

Discretionary Security and Non-Security Spending

The G. W. Bush and Obama Administrations have each created their own division of security and non-security discretionary spending as a way of communicating their budgetary priorities. The Obama and Bush Administration budgets have presented summaries of discretionary funding that split out security spending from non-security spending.[102] Unlike the division of discretionary spending into the categories of domestic, international, and defense, which has become routine in budget analyses, several ways of dividing security spending from non-security spending have been used. In particular, the G. W. Bush and Obama Administration definitions vary in significant ways.

The Budget Control Act of 2011 includes two definitions of security spending: an original definition (explained below) and a revised definition corresponding to the national defense budget function (050) and non-defense (all other programs).[103] These BCA security categories set up "firewalls" to ensure that reductions in security spending cannot be used to fund increases in non-security spending, and vice versa. The American Taxpayer Relief Act of 2012 (ATRA) switched FY2013 caps to security/non-security from defense/nondefense.[104]

What Is "Homeland Security" or "Security" Spending?

Any division of spending into security and non-security components would likely present conceptual and practical difficulties.[105] Moreover, the widely used term "homeland security," which comprises some but not all non-defense security spending, does not already readily translate in budgetary categories.[106] **Figure 5** provides a schematic view of the relationship between defense spending (budget function 050) and security spending as defined in the Budget Control Act. That definition nearly coincides with the security definition used by the Obama Administration. The Obama Administration has defined security spending as funding for

- Department of Defense-Military;
- Department of Energy's National Nuclear Security Administration;
- International Affairs (function 150; includes State Department and U.S. AID);[107]
- Department of Homeland Security; and
- Department of Veterans Affairs.[108]

The Budget Control Act of 2011 (BCA), in addition to items on that list, includes the Intelligence Community Management Account, which is far smaller than the other items. The BCA "revised security" category for discretionary spending, as noted above, is national defense (budget function 050) and non-defense (everything else).

Activities within budget subfunction 053 (Atomic Energy Defense Activities), aside from the National Nuclear Security Administration (NNSA) by this definition are classed as non-security. While the G. W. Bush Administration defined parts of the Department of Homeland Security within its "security" classification, the Obama Administration includes all of that department's funding.

The G. W. Bush Administration defined security funding as spending on the "Department of Defense, Homeland Security activities Government-wide; and International Affairs."[109] The Obama Administration includes funding for the Department of Veterans Affairs and excludes Justice Department agencies such as the Federal Bureau of Investigation (FBI) under its security rubric, while the Bush Administration's definition included the FBI and other law enforcement bureaus and excluded the Department of Veterans Affairs.

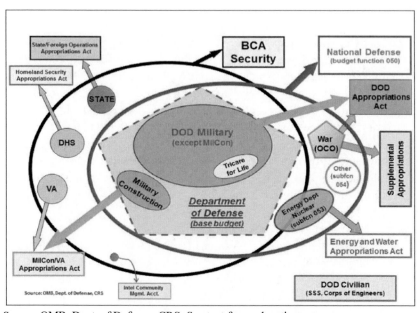

Source: OMB, Dept. of Defense, CRS. See text for explanations.

Figure 5. How Defense and Security Intersect: A Schematic View.

Most homeland security spending, by either definition, takes place in the Department of Defense, the Department of Homeland Security, and the Department of Energy. Many other federal agencies spend at least some portion of their budget on what are arguably homeland security tasks, so that a significant amount of homeland security spending takes place in agencies and programs whose primary focus is not security oriented. Some federal activities, such as Coast Guard patrols and research at the Centers for Disease Control and Prevention, advance interests clearly linked to security objectives as well as those which are not. Moreover, some federal programs tasked with non-security aims in normal times may respond to specific homeland security challenges. These issues complicate budgetary analyses of homeland security spending.

The President's budget submission must report homeland security spending.[110] This definition, drawn more narrowly than "security," can exclude some DOD activities not closely tied to security concerns, such as military bands, while including certain non-DOD activities such as National Institutes of Health research on countermeasures against chemical or biological weapons. OMB's security spending estimates are based on reports from 32 agencies with homeland security responsibilities. Those agencies provide OMB with budget reports that provide a level of detail unavailable in publicly available data.

Trends in "Security" and "Non-Security" Discretionary Spending

Figure 6 shows trends in discretionary spending, divided into defense, non-defense security, and non-security categories in terms of budget authority, while **Figure 7** shows the same categories in terms of outlays. Because budget authority can translate into outlays that stretch over several years, changes in outlays tend to be more gradual.

For example, a spike in non-defense security spending for 2005, reflecting disaster spending following Hurricane Katrina and other catastrophic events, appears in the budget authority figure, but not in the outlays figure. Similarly, the spending spike reflecting Recovery Act spending is narrower for BA than for outlays.

Trends in non-defense security spending can also be decomposed to show how its components have changed over time. **Figure 8** shows outlays for non-defense security spending programs since 1976.[111]

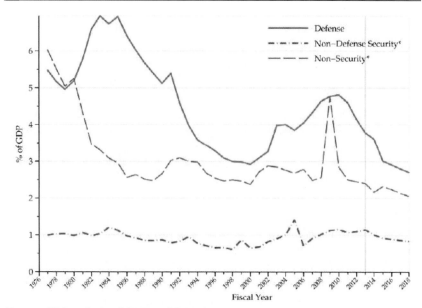

Source: CRS analysis of OMB and BEA data.

Notes: The security category reflects BCA original definition, except that war funding (OCO) is included. Defense here includes Dept. of Defense-Military spending. Non-defense security includes Dept. of Energy's National Nuclear Security Admin., International Affairs (function 150), Dept. of Homeland Security and Dept. of Veterans Affairs, and Intelligence Community Management account. FY2012 values estimated; FY2013-FY2018 levels requested by the President. Historical data reflect certain OMB imputations.

Figure 6. Discretionary Budget Authority by Security Category; FY1976-FY2018, as a Percentage of GDP.

Non-defense security programs have been affected by a wide range of policy developments. International program spending fell in the 1980s and 1990s, but rose sharply after the events of September 11, 2001. Spending on federal operations now contained within DHS also increased dramatically after that date. The costs of discretionary veterans' programs also have risen rapidly in the past decade, although more driven by the aging of Korean War and Vietnam War era veterans and expanded access to VA medical care. Only a small part of the increase in VA discretionary costs is due to the costs of treating veterans from the wars in Afghanistan and Iraq.[112]

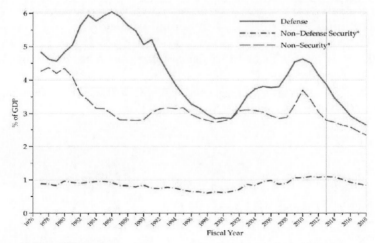

Source: OMB and BEA.
Note: See notes for Figure 6.

Figure 7. Discretionary Outlays by Security; FY1976-FY2018, as a Percentage of GDP.

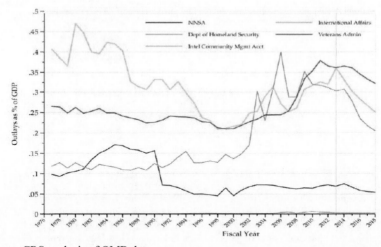

Source: CRS analysis of OMB data.
Notes: Dept. of Defense-Military is budget function 051; NNSA is the Dept. of Energy's National Nuclear Security Administration; International Affairs are function 150; DHS is the Dept. of Homeland Security. FY2013 values estimated; FY2014-FY2018 are President's requested levels.

Figure 8. Non-Defense Security Outlays by Component; BCA Definition; as a Percentage of GDP, FY1976-FY2018.

Discretionary Spending by Functional Category

Federal activities are classified among budget functions. Analyzing trends by budget function provides a more detailed view of how federal spending has evolved. **Figure 9** shows average annual changes in discretionary spending for the last three decades and for FY2011-FY2017.[113]

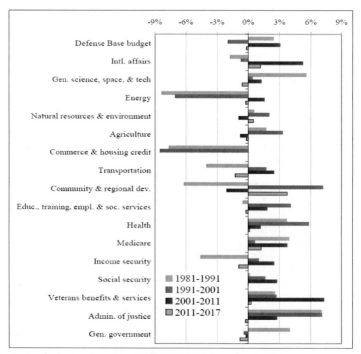

Source: CRS calculations based on FY2013 OMB data and projections.

Notes: Values for FY2011-FY2017 incorporate OMB projections that presume the Administration's proposals for FY2013-FY2017 are adopted. The Administration proposes modifications to BCA as part of a package of budgetary changes. All years are fiscal years. The budgetary treatment of federal credit programs changed in 1990, affects comparisons of programs that include loans and loan guarantees. See CRS Report R42632, *Budgetary Treatment of Federal Credit (Direct Loans and Loan Guarantees): Concepts, History, and Issues for the 112th Congress*, by James M. Bickley. Budget function data were designed to reflect funding for policy objectives across various agencies. For example, the Department of Homeland Security includes programs that fall within many budget functions, including Transportation, Administration of Justice, Community and Regional Development.

Figure 9. Average Growth Rates for Discretionary BA by Subfunction; Average Annual Percentage Change by Decade and for FY2011-FY2017.

Spending in some policy areas, such as community and regional development, agriculture, natural resources and environment, and general government, has grown very slowly or has been cut. Spending in other areas, such as war costs, veterans' programs, international affairs, and Medicare administration, has expanded rapidly in the last decade.[114] Unless this trend is restrained or reversed, security-related non-defense spending could displace funding for other non-defense programs. Similarly, protecting non-defense programs that have benefited from broad bipartisan support could lead to deeper reductions in less prominent programs.

CONCLUSION: IS THE DECLINING SHARE OF DISCRETIONARY SPENDING A PROBLEM?

While discretionary spending, which chiefly funds the operations of federal agencies, accounts for about two-sevenths of federal outlays, it has been at the center of efforts to restrain federal spending. In addition, long-term trends—to large extent baby-boom demographics and health care costs—have helped tilt federal spending towards mandatory programs. Under current law, discretionary spending is projected to shrink to 24% of federal outlays by FY2023.[115] In that year, discretionary spending is projected at $1.4 trillion (current dollars).

While the federal deficit is projected to fall in FY2014 and FY2015, higher interest costs and mandatory spending are expected to increase fiscal pressures in later years. For example, in FY2023, the federal deficit is projected to rise $900 billion. Closing the gap between federal spending and receipts through reductions in discretionary spending, therefore, may be difficult.

The shift toward mandatory spending and away from discretionary spending may raise concerns for two reasons. First, as the portion of the federal budget controlled on a year-by-year basis shrinks, making adjustments in spending levels may become more difficult. Mandatory spending, which requires changes in authorizing legislation, is not normally considered on an annual basis. Moreover, existing budget enforcement mechanisms are largely designed to constrain discretionary spending, while measures that can be used to reduce mandatory spending have been more difficult to apply in recent years.

Second, the rise of mandatory programs' share of federal spending reflects an aging population. Policymakers may choose to adapt the structure of the federal budget to reflect the needs of a growing segment of retired or elderly Americans. Such shifts in resource allocation, however, could affect intergenerational equity and the federal government's ability to respond to the needs of future generations.

APPENDIX. DEFENSE AND NON-DEFENSE SPENDING, FY1977-FY2012

Table A-1 shows National Defense (budget function 050) and Non-Defense (all other) spending (BA) in current dollars and in constant FY2012 dollars (i.e., adjusted for inflation). These figures exclude funding for the Iraq and Afghan wars and related activities.

Table A-1. National Defense and Non-Defense Spending, FY1977-FY2012

National Defense without Afghan and Iraq Wars			Non-Defense without Afghan and Iraq Wars		
In Billions of Dollars of Budget Authority			In Billions of Dollars of Budget Authority		
Fiscal Year	In Current $	In $FY2012	Fiscal Year	In Current $	In $FY2012
1977	110.4	340.6	1977	136.5	421.1
1978	117.3	339.3	1978	142.6	412.3
1979	126.9	339.5	1979	149.1	399.0
1980	144.5	355.3	1980	166.7	409.9
1981	180.4	403.8	1981	160.5	359.2
1982	217.2	454.9	1982	138.4	289.9
1983	245.0	491.6	1983	143.3	287.6
1984	265.6	513.9	1984	158.1	305.8
1985	294.9	552.6	1985	161.7	303.1
1986	289.6	530.5	1986	148.3	271.6
1987	288.0	513.7	1987	157.8	281.5
1988	292.5	505.6	1988	160.8	277.9
1989	300.1	499.3	1989	171.0	284.6
1990	303.9	487.8	1990	192.8	309.4
1991	332.2	513.7	1991	213.9	330.7
1992	299.1	450.8	1992	232.3	350.1
1993	276.1	407.2	1993	247.2	364.5
1994	262.2	378.7	1994	250.3	361.5

National Defense without Afghan and Iraq Wars			Non-Defense without Afghan and Iraq Wars		
In Billions of Dollars of Budget Authority			In Billions of Dollars of Budget Authority		
1995	262.9	371.8	1995	238.5	337.3
1996	265.2	367.9	1996	235.8	327.1
1997	266.2	362.7	1997	245.0	333.7
1998	272.4	366.4	1998	257.2	346.0
1999	288.3	382.8	1999	293.5	389.7
2000	300.8	391.5	2000	283.6	369.2
2001	313.4	398.6	2001	332.1	422.4
2002	346.2	433.1	2002	373.1	466.9
2003	377.6	463.0	2003	390.7	479.1
2004	413.3	494.2	2004	401.1	479.6
2005	397.2	460.1	2005	482.7	559.0
2006	439.7	492.5	2006	435.5	487.8
2007	457.5	497.7	2007	443.9	482.8
2008	506.7	538.8	2008	487.3	518.2
2009	546.7	573.0	2009	790.2	828.2
2010	551.9	573.3	2010	538.0	558.7
2011	552.2	562.2	2011	498.0	507.2
2012	554.3	554.3	2012	489.0	489.0

Sources: OMB and CBO.

Notes: Deflated with OMB's GDP price index. War funding estimates from CRS Report RL33110, *The Cost of Iraq, Afghanistan, and Other Global War on Terror Operations Since 9/!!*, by Amy Belasco.

End Notes

[1] Annual appropriations acts fall within the jurisdiction of the House and Senate Appropriations Committees.

[2] Exceptions exist. For example, salaries for Members of Congress, the President, and federal judges are classified as mandatory spending, as are essentially all federal retirement and disability costs. Direct spending is controlled by committees with legislative jurisdiction.

[3] While federal officials often have some discretion to choose how quickly appropriated funds are spent, they face constraints imposed by legislation designed to protect Congress's power of the purse. According to the Anti-Deficiency Act, a federal official cannot spend government money beyond what is available through appropriations or a fund by law. See Government Accountability Office, *Antideficiency Act Background*, available at http://www.gao.gov/ada/antideficiency.htm for code citations and explanations. The Congressional Budget Act and Impoundment Control Act of 1974 (P.L. 93-344) limits the ability of federal officials to withhold or delay spending of appropriated funds without Congressional approval.

[4] Office of Management and Budget (OMB), *Mid Session Review*, Table S-5, July 2013, available at http://www.whitehouse.gov/sites/default/files/omb/budget/fy2014/assets/14msr.pdf. Total federal outlays, according to preliminary final financial results for FY2013, were $3,454 billion, about $82 billion less than the Mid Session Review estimate. A breakdown of spending by Budget Enforcement Act (BEA) categories, however, was not provided in those preliminary final results. See U.S. Treasury, "Joint Statement of Secretary Lew and OMB Director Burwell on Budget Results for Fiscal Year 2013," October 30, 2013, available at http://www.treasury.gov/press-center/press-releases/ Pages/jl2197.aspx.

[5] These categories are called BEA categories in some Office of Management and Budget (OMB) publications, because they are defined in the Budget Enforcement Act of 1990 (P.L. 101-508).

[6] The Government Accountability Office (GAO) notes that "A mandatory program is simply one that Congress directs (rather than merely authorizes) the agency to conduct, but within the limits of available funding." *Principles of Federal Appropriations Law* (Red Book), GAO-040261SP, vol. 1, p. 3-52. For an overview of mandatory spending trends, see CRS Report RL33074, *Mandatory Spending Since 1962*, by Mindy R. Levit and D. Andrew Austin.

[7] For an overview, see CRS Report 98-721, *Introduction to the Federal Budget Process*, coordinated by Bill Heniff Jr.

[8] CRS Report RS20129, *Entitlements and Appropriated Entitlements in the Federal Budget Process*, by Bill Heniff Jr. For one listing of permanent appropriations, see GAO, *Inventory of Accounts With Spending Authority and Permanent Appropriations, 1997*, OGC-98-23, January 19, 1998, available at http://www.gao.gov/assets/230/225159.pdf.

[9] Monetary policy, which affects the money supply, interest rates, and credit conditions, is another key instrument of macroeconomic management.

[10] Estimates of the magnitude of stimulus effects vary. For a review of the literature, see CRS Report RL33657, *Running Deficits: Positives and Pitfalls*, by D. Andrew Austin.

[11] A recession occurs when an economy contracts. See National Bureau of Economic Research, "The NBER's Business Cycle Dating Committee," available at http://www.nber.org/cycles/recessions.html.

[12] CBO, *The Effects of Automatic Stabilizers on the Federal Budget as of 2013*, March 8, 2013, available at http://www.cbo.gov/publication/43977.

[13] Peter R. Orszag, "History Shows U.S. Can Stimulate Now, Cut Later," Bloomberg.com, May 22, 2012, available at http://www.cfr.org/geoeconomics/history-shows-us-can-stimulate-now-cut-later/p28338.

[14] The original CBO score of ARRA is available at http://www.cbo.gov/sites/default/files/cbofiles/ftpdocs/99xx/ doc9989/hr1conference.pdf.

[15] Certain Supplemental Nutrition Assistance Program (SNAP) benefits were cut by P.L. 111-226 (H.R. 1546). For details, see CRS Report R41374, *Reducing SNAP (Food Stamp) Benefits Provided by the ARRA: P.L. 111-226 and P.L. 111-296*, by Randy Alison Aussenberg, Jim Monke, and Gene Falk; and CBO, "Budgetary Effects of Senate Amendment 4575," cost estimate, August 4, 2010, available at http://www.cbo.gov /ftpdocs/117xx/doc11756/sa4575.pdf.

[16] U.S. Congressional Budget Office, *Budget and Economic Outlook*, January 2012, Box 1-1, available at http://www.cbo.gov/sites/default/files/cbofiles/attachments/01-31-2012_Outlook.pdf.

[17] IMF, *World Economic Outlook: Coping with High Debt and Sluggish Growth*, October 2012, available at http://www.imf.org/external/pubs/ft/weo/2012/02/pdf/text.pdf.

[18] See Carmen M. Reinhart and Kenneth S. Rogoff, *This Time is Different: Eight Centuries of Financial Folly*, (Princeton, 2009); and "Sorry, U.S. Recoveries Really Aren't Different," Bloomberg News, October 15, 2012, available at http://www.bloomberg.com/news/2012-10-15/sorry-u-s-recoveries-really-aren-t-different.html.

[19] Christina Romer, "Not My Father's Recession: The Extraordinary Challenges and Policy Responses of the First Twenty Months of the Obama Administration," remarks at the National Press Club, September 1, 2010, available at http://www.whitehouse.gov/sites/default/files/microsites/100901-National-Press-Club.pdf.

[20] Kenneth Rogoff, "Why America Isn't Working," Project Syndicate, September 1, 2010, available at http://www.project-syndicate.org/commentary/rogoff72/English.

[21] IMF, World Economic Outlook: Coping with High Debt and Sluggish Growth, October 2012, available at http://www.imf.org/external/pubs/ft/weo/2012/02/pdf/text.pdf. See discussion in Box 1.1 written by IMF chief economist Olivier Blanchard and Daniel Leigh (pp. 41-43).

[22] Forecasters surveyed by the Blue Chip Economic Indicators review on average expected growth of 2.8% in 2014 (fourth quarter over fourth quarter), while current estimates put 2013 growth at 1.8%. See *Blue Chip Economic Indicators*, January 10, 2014. Also see Oliver Blanchard, "Recovery Strengthening, but Much Work Remains," IMF Direct, January 21, 2014, available at http://blog-imfdirect.imf.org/2014/01/21/recovery-strengthening-but-much-workremains/.

[23] Kris Dawsey and Hui Shan, "Housing Sector Jobs Poised for a Comeback," Goldman Sachs US Daily, February 11, 2013; Mark Zandi, "U.S. Macro Outlook: Restarting the Engines," Moody's Analytics Dismal Scientist Blog, February 6, 2013, available at http://www.economy.com/dismal/article_free.asp?cid=237408&tid=5FCB4BBF-D759-422DBD25-BFF7D505D457.

[24] For example, see Claire Jones, "Too Early to Declare Crisis Over, says Draghi," *Financial Times*, January 9, 2014; Joe Zhang, "Rising Rates Will Help Cure China's Credit Addiction," *Financial Times*, January 12, 2014.

[25] For details, see Congressional Research Service, "The Budget Control Act and Alternate Defense and Non-Defense Spending Paths, FY2012-FY2021," by Amy Belasco and Andrew Austin, November 16, 2012, available from authors. This comparison is made in terms of budget authority. Before passage of ATRA, BCA provisions were slated to bring discretionary base defense spending to its FY2007 level and non-defense spending to near its level in FY2003 or FY2004. Inflation adjustments made using GDP price index.

[26] CBO, "Letter to the Honorable John A. Boehner and the Honorable Harry Reid Estimating the Impact on the Deficit of the Budget Control Act of 2011," August 1, 2011, available at http://www.cbo.gov/ftpdocs/124xx/doc12414/09-12- BudgetControlAct.pdf.

[27] For an analysis of the provisions of the BCA, see CRS Report R41965, *The Budget Control Act of 2011*, by Bill Heniff Jr., Elizabeth Rybicki, and Shannon M. Mahan. For details on debt limit provisions, see CRS Report RL31967, *The Debt Limit: History and Recent Increases*, by D. Andrew Austin and Mindy R. Levit.

[28] For two versions of the negotiations that led to the BCA, see Peter Wallsten et al., "Obama's Evolution: Behind the Failed 'Grand Bargain' on the Debt," *Washington Post*, March 17, 2012, p. A1, available at http://www.washingtonpost.com/politics/obamas-evolution-behind-the-failed-grand-bargain-on-the-debt/2012/03/15/gIQAHyyfJS_story.html; Matthew Bai, "Obama vs. Boehner: Who Killed the Debt Deal?" *New York Times Magazine*, March 28, 2012, p. MM22, available at http://www.nytimes.com/2012/04/01 /magazine/obama-vs-boehner-who-killedthe-debt-deal.html.

[29] Amounts above cap levels would be sequestered as specified in Balanced Budget and Emergency Deficit Control Act of 1985 (BBEDCA; P.L. 99-177, as amended), §251(a)(1). A sequester would affect budgetary resources in addition to new budget authority as well, such as defense unobligated balances. Non-exempted mandatory programs would continue to be sequestered from FY2014 to FY2021 under provisions of the BCA.

[30] H.J.Res. 117 passed on a 329-91 vote in the House on September 13, 2012, and passed on a 62-30 vote in the Senate on September 22.

[31] See CRS Report R42647, *Continuing Resolutions: Overview of Components and Recent Practices*, by Jessica Tollestrup.

[32] CBO, "Budget authority subject to $1,407 (sic) billion cap: CR as introduced," September 2012.

[33] BBEDCA (P.L. 99-177), §251(a)(1). For details, see House Appropriations Committee Ranking Member Norman Dicks, "A Report on the Consequences of Sequestration," Dear Colleague Letter, October 9, 2012, available at http://www.naph.org/Links/ADV/House-Sequestration-Letter-10-9-12.aspx. Also see Amy Belasco and D. Andrew Austin, *The Budget Control Act and Alternate Defense and Non-Defense Spending Paths, FY2012-FY2021*, congressional distribution memorandum, available from authors.

[34] For details, see CRS Report R42949, *The American Taxpayer Relief Act of 2012: Modifications to the Budget Enforcement Procedures in the Budget Control Act*, by Bill Heniff Jr.

[35] Thus the size of the FY2013 sequester was reduced by $24 billion.

[36] See CBO, "Estimate of the Budgetary Effects of H.R. 8, the American Taxpayer Relief Act of 2012, as passed by the Senate on January 1, 2013," January 1, 2013, available at http://www.cbo.gov/sites/default/files/cbofiles/attachments/American%20Taxpayer%20Relief%20Act.pdf.

[37] BBEDCA (P.L. 99-177), §251(a)(1) states that "(w)ithin 15 calendar days after Congress adjourns to end a session, there shall be a sequestration to eliminate a budget-year breach, if any, within any category."

[38] The definition of the security and non-security categories is explained in more detail below.

[39] Jeffrey D. Zients, Acting OMB Director, letter to President Barack Obama, March 27, 2013.

[40] CBO, *Budget and Economic Outlook*, February 2013, Table 1-4, available at http://www.cbo.gov/sites/default/files/ cbofiles/attachments/43907-BudgetOutlook.pdf.

[41] For details, see CRS Report R42894, *An Overview of the Tax Provisions in the American Taxpayer Relief Act of 2012* , by Margot L. Crandall-Hollick; CRS Report R42884, *The "Fiscal Cliff" and the American Taxpayer Relief Act of 2012*, coordinated by Mindy R. Levit.

[42] CBO, *Economic Effects of Policies Contributing to Fiscal Tightening in 2013*, November 8, 2012; Alex Phillips, "And Now, on to the Fiscal Cliff," Goldman Sachs Global Economics, Commodities and Strategy Research U.S. Daily, November 7, 2012.

[43] CRS Report R42700, *The "Fiscal Cliff": Macroeconomic Consequences of Tax Increases and Spending Cuts*, by Jane G. Gravelle.

[44] For example, see H.R. 3662, "Amending the Balanced Budget and Emergency Deficit Control Act," December 14, 2011, available at http://armedservices.house.gov/index.cfm /files/serve?File_id=71803a67-5d45-4bfa-88b9- 80c6f5b42d82k2. See also U.S. Congress, House Budget Committee, *Hearing on the 2011 Budget Control Act and Potential Sequestration*, 112th Cong., 2nd sess., April 25, 2012. Also see U.S. Congress, Senate Committee on Appropriations, *The Impacts of Sequestration*, 113th Cong., 1st sess., February 14, 2013 (documents available at http://www.appropriations.senate.gov/ht-

full.cfm?method=hearings.view&id=17d3dc99-c065-4bec-a7c8-   cfd374bf41a3);   U.S. Congress, Senate Committee on Armed Services, *Impacts of Sequestration and/or CR*, 113th Cong., 1st sess., February 12, 2013 (documents available at http://www.armed-services.senate.gov/hearings/event.cfm? eventid=75b85d4058863364782faf917d08a08a).

[45] H.Con.Res. 112, §201, §202.

[46] CBO, "Sequester Replacement Reconciliation Act," Letter to Rep. David Drier, May 9, 2012, available at http://www.cbo.gov/publication/43234.

[47] See "Summary of Changes between H.R. 6684 and H.R. 5652," December 19, 2012, available at http://www.rules.house.gov/Media/file/PDF_112_2/PDF/HR6684SummChang.pdf.

[48] See Steven Dennis and Humberto Sanchez, "Coburn Blocks Attempt to Bring Up Bill to Replace Sequester," CQ News, April 23, 2013.

[49] For currently proposed OCO amounts, see Table 3 on p. 7 of the OMB FY2014 sequestration preview   report,   available   at   http://www.whitehouse.gov/sites/default/files   /omb /assets/legislative_reports/fy14_preview_and_joint_committee_reductions_reports_ 04102013.pdf. The FY2014 amount is sum of $88,482 million (OCO in budget function 050) and $3,807 million (OCO in international affairs).

[50] White House, Office of the Press Secretary, "Averting the Sequester and Finding a Balanced Approach to Deficit Reduction," February 8, 2013, available at http://www.whitehouse.gov /the-press-office/2013/02/08/averting-sequesterand-finding-balanced-approach-deficit-reduction.

[51] See OMB, *Report to the Congress on the Joint Committee Sequestration for Fiscal Year 2013*, March   1,   2013,   http://www.whitehouse.gov/sites/default/files/omb/assets/legislative_ reports/fy13ombjcsequestrationreport.pdf.

[52] Ibid., Table 2, p. 4.

[53] Karen Parrish, "Panetta: Fiscal Crisis Poses Biggest Immediate Threat to DOD," American Forces Press Service, January 10, 2014, available at http://www.defense.gov/News /newsarticle.aspx?ID=118974.

[54] Ibid., Table 3, pp. 6.

[55] BBEDCA Section 256. See CRS Report R42051, *Budget Control Act: Potential Impact of Sequestration on Health Reform Spending*, by C. Stephen Redhead.

[56] CBO, letter to Senator Sessions, March 12, 2013, available at http://www.cbo.gov/sites /default/files/cbofiles/ attachments/Sessions_Sequester_CR.pdf. Note that FY2013 outlays estimates may change to reflect details of the OMB sequestration order of March 1, 2013.

[57] H.R. 933, Section 1101 specifies an 0.16% across-the-board rescission the Department of the Interior, Environment, and Related Agencies; a 0.189% across-the-board rescission the Departments of Labor, Health and Human Services, and Education, and Related Agencies. In addition, a 0.109% rescission would apply to security programs (as defined in the BCA) and a 0.0098% rescission in non-security programs (Section 3001).

[58] See H.R. 933, Section 3002.

[59] Senator Barbara Mikulski, floor statement, March 12, 2013, text available at http://www.appropriations.senate.gov/ news.cfm?method=news.view&id=5c19a6a3-4263-4cb6-99a6-38517e1cb00f.

[60] For House version, see CBO, Total Discretionary Appropriations for FY2013, Including H.R. 933, the Department of Defense, Military Construction and Veterans Affairs, and Full-Year Continuing Appropriations Act, 2013 as Introduced on March 4, 2013, and P.L. 113-2, the Disaster   Relief   Appropriations   Act,   2013,   March   4,   2013,   available   at https://www.cbo.gov/sites/default/files/cbofiles/attachments/hr933.pdf.

For Senate version, see CBO, *Total Discretionary Appropriations for Fiscal Year 2013, Including the Consolidated and Continuing Appropriations Act, 2013 (an Amendment in the Nature of a Substitute to H.R. 933) as Posted on the Senate Committee on Appropriations Web Site on March 11, 2013 and Public Law 113-2, the Disaster Relief Appropriations Act, 2013*, March 12, 2013, available at https://www.cbo.gov/sites/default/files /cbofiles /attachments/ hr933AmendmentintheNatureofaSubstitute.pdf.

[61] OMB, *FY2014 Budget of the U.S. Government*, p. 45. See Table 6 of memorandum cited below for $800 billion estimate for difference between BCA revised caps and lowered caps.

[62] According to the FY2014 *Mid Session Review*, "(t)he 2014 Budget includes allowances, similar to the Function 920 allowances used in Budget Resolutions, to represent amounts to be allocated among the respective agencies to reach the proposed defense and non-defense caps for 2015 and beyond. These levels are determined for illustrative purposes but do not reflect specific policy decisions." See fn. 5, to Table S-10, p. 58, available at http://www.whitehouse.gov/sites/ default/files/omb/budget/fy2014/assets/14msr.pdf.

[63] See CBO, "FY 2014 House Current Status of Discretionary Appropriations as of August 1, 2013," available at http://www.cbo.gov/sites/default/files/cbofiles/attachments/44333_BY 2014House_8-1.pdf; and OMB Sequestration Preview Report (cited above). CBO estimated that the Homeland Security bill would include a $5.6 billion disaster funding adjustment.

[64] That Senate total excluded adjustments to caps for war funding (OCO), disaster funding, program integrity, and emergency items. With those adjustments, the Senate total for FY2014 appropriations at the end of July 2013 was $1,149.6 billion. See CBO, "FY 2014 Senate Current Status of Discretionary Appropriations as of August 2, 2013," available at http://www.cbo.gov/sites/default/files/cbofiles/attachments/44399_BY2014_Senate_8-2.pdf.

[65] For details, see CRS Report R43338, *Congressional Action on FY2014 Appropriations Measures*, by Jessica Tollestrup.

[66] That total excludes adjustments for war funding (OCO), disaster funding, program integrity, and emergency items. Annualized funding reflecting those adjustments totaled $1,087.7 billion. See CBO, "CBO Estimate of the Continuing Appropriations Act, 2014, as Introduced in the Senate on October 16, 2013, as an Amendment to H.R. 2775," October 16, 2013, available at http://www.cbo.gov/sites/default/files/cbofiles/attachments/ ContinuingAppropriationsAct2014.pdf.

[67] The defense category (National Defense budget function (050)) is called the "revised security category" in the BCA and the Bipartisan Budget Act of 2013. The non-defense category is called the "revised nonsecurity category."

[68] BBEDCA Sec. 251A (2 U.S.C. 901a) directs OMB to lower the revised spending caps for FY2014-FY2021. Section 101 of the Bipartisan Budget Act of 2013 requires that the lowering of caps "shall not be implemented for fiscal years 2014 and 2015."

[69] CRS calculations based on CBO and OMB data.

[70] CBO, "2014 Discretionary Appropriations Including H.R. 3547, as Posted on House Rules Website on January 13, Excluding OCO, Disaster, Prog. Int. and Emergencies," January 14, 2014. H.R. 3547, originally named the "Space Launch Liability Indemnification Extension Act," was used as the legislative vehicle for the final FY2014 appropriations act.

[71] 31 U.S.C. 11, §1105.

[72] "WH: Obama to Propose Fiscal 2015 Budget One Month Late," United Press International (UPI), January 23, 2014; http://www.upi.com/Top_News/US/2014/01/23/WH-Obama-to-propose-Fiscal-2015-budget-one-month-late/UPI30221390502663/.

[73] Marcus Weisgerber, "2015 US Budget Proposal Not Likely Until Late February," *Defense News*, Jan. 6, 2014, http://www.defensenews.com/article/20140106/DEFREG02/301060022 /2015-US-Budget-Proposal-Not-Likely-UntilLate-February. In normal budget cycles, OMB reviews agency proposals and issues "passback" guidance in late November. For the FY2015 budget cycle, according to quoted sources, the "passback" guidance would occur in January 2014.

[74] Sylvia Burwell, OMB Director,*FY2015 Budget Guidance*, memorandum M-13-14,May 29, 2013, available at http://www.whitehouse.gov/sites/default/files/omb/memoranda/2013/m-13-14.pdf.

[75] "Secretary of the Treasury Lew Delivers Remarks on the U.S. Economy at the Council on Foreign Relations," *CQ Financial Transcripts*, January 16, 2014.

[76] "CBO to Release Budget and Economic Outlook on February 4," *CBO blog*, January 22, 2014, available at http://www.cbo.gov/publication/45034.

[77] These categories are defined in the Budget Enforcement Act (P.L. 101-508).

[78] OMB, FY2014 *Mid Session Review*, Table S-4, July 2013.

[79] CBO, *Budget Projections—May 2013*, May 14, 2013, available at http://www.cbo.gov /publication/44195. Years in this report refer to federal fiscal years unless otherwise noted. Since 1977, federal fiscal years have started on October 1. Figures for FY1962-FY1968 from U.S. Office of Management and Budget, *Budget for FY2014*, *Historical Tables*, available at http://www.whitehouse.gov/omb/budget/Historicals/. Figures for FY1969 and beyond from the U.S. Congressional Budget Office, *Historical Tables*, available at http://www.cbo.gov/sites/default/files/cbofiles/ attachments/HistoricalBudget Data.xls.

[80] For one analysis of the effects of abrupt changes in retirement benefits, see Andries De Grip, Maarten Lindeboom, and Raymond M. Montizaan, "Shattered Dreams: The Effects of Changing the Pension System Late in the Game," *Economic Journal*, vol. 122, pp. 1-25, 2012.

[81] For additional discussion, see CRS Report RL33623, *Long-Term Measures of Fiscal Imbalance*, by D. Andrew Austin.

[82] For details, see CRS Report RL33110, *The Cost of Iraq, Afghanistan, and Other Global War on Terror Operations Since 9/11*, by Amy Belasco.

[83] Inflation adjustments calculated using GDP price index. Prices for some categories of goods and services purchased by the government, such as health care, tend to rise faster than the overall price level. Maintaining current levels of government services will require funding levels that increase faster than the overall price level, as measured by the GDP price index. Figure does not reflect changes in ATRA (FY2013 caps reduced by $4 billion, FY2014 caps reduced by $8 billion) or the supplemental funding (P.L. 113-2) for disaster relief for damage caused by Hurricane Sandy (scored at $41.7 billion in emergency-designated budget authority). See discussion about of FY2013 full-year funding measures for budget scoring information.

[84] For an account written by President Reagan's first budget director, see David A. Stockman, *The Triumph of Politics*, (New York: Harper & Row, 1986).

[85] This section draws upon contributions from Amy Belasco, CRS Specialist in U.S. Defense Policy and Budget.

[86] See CRS Report RS22926, *Costs of Major U.S. Wars*, by Stephen Daggett, Table 1, note b.

[87] For details, see CRS Report RL33110, *The Cost of Iraq, Afghanistan, and Other Global War on Terror Operations Since 9/11*, by Amy Belasco; and CRS Report R40682, *Troop Levels in the Afghan and Iraq Wars, FY2001-FY2012: Cost and Other Potential Issues*, by Amy Belasco.

[88] See Figure 1 in CRS Report R42334, *A Historical Perspective on "Hollow Forces,"* by Andrew Feickert and Stephen Daggett.

[89] See Table 1 in CRS Report RS22926, *Costs of Major U.S. Wars*, by Stephen Daggett.

[90] RAND, *The Evolution of the All-Volunteer Force*, issue brief, 2006; available at http://www.rand.org/content/dam/ rand/pubs/research_briefs/2006/RAND_RB9195.pdf. For an analysis of the full economic costs of the draft, see Walter Oi, "The Economic Cost of the Draft," *American Economic Review* vol. 27, no. 2 (1967), pp. 39-62.

[91] Scott Wilson and David Nakamura, "Obama Announces Reduced U.S. Role in Afghanistan Starting this Spring," *Washington Post*, January 11, 2013.

[92] Defense discretionary spending includes enacted supplemental requests. OMB, *Budget for Fiscal Year 2011, Historical Tables*, Table 8.2, available at http://www.whitehouse.gov /omb/budget/Historicals/. 2010 spending includes proposed $41.1 billion supplemental appropriation.

[93] *New York Times*, October 22, 2007. Transcript available at http://www.nytimes.com/2007 /10/22/washington/ 22mullen-text.html.

[94] Testimony of CBO Assistant Director J. Michael Gilmore, in U.S. Congress, House Budget Committee, *The 2009 Future Years Defense Program: Implications and Alternatives*, hearings, 111th Cong., 1st sess., February 4, 2009; Testimony of CRS Specialist in Defense Policy and Budgets Stephen Daggett, in U.S. Congress, House Budget Committee, *Sustainability of Current Defense Plans*, hearings, 111th Cong., 1st sess., February 4, 2009.

[95] U.S. Secretary of Defense, Memorandum for Secretaries of the Military Departments, OSD 09637-10, August 16, 2010.

[96] Secretary of Defense, Leon Panetta, "Letter to Senator McCain and Senator Lindsey Graham," November 14, 2011; http://www.politico.com/static/PPM205_11_14_11_panetta_respsonse_to_mccain_graham_ltr.html (sic).

[97] Deputy Secretary of Defense Ashton B. Carter, Memorandum on Handling Budgetary Uncertainty in Fiscal Year 2013, January 10, 2013.

[98] Michael O'Hanlon, "What Cutting Defense Really Means," *Wall Street Journal*, January 30, 2013, p. A13. See also Gordon Adams, "Behind the Rhetoric: The Pentagon Starts to Manage the Defense Drawdown," *Foreign Policy*, January 15, 2013, available at http://www.foreignpolicy.com/articles/2013/01/15/behind_the_rhetoric.

[99] For one view of the federal budget during the first years of the Reagan Administration, see David Stockman, *The Triumph of Politics* (New York: Harper&Row, 1986), pp. 401-411.

[100] CBO, *Budget Projections—May 2013*, May 14, 2013, available at http://www.cbo.gov /publication/44195.

[101] For instance, the Budget Enforcement Act of 1990 (P.L. 101-508) set separate caps on defense, domestic, and international spending through 1993, with caps on total spending for later years.

[102] For details, see U.S. Office of Management and Budget, *Budget of the U.S. Government, FY2009*, Tables S-2 and S4, and the "Homeland Security Funding Analysis" chapter in the *Analytic Perspectives* volume. In circular A-11, OMB defines federal homeland security activities as those that "focus on combating and protecting against terrorism, and that occur within the United States and its territories or outside of the United States and its territories if they support domestically-based systems or activities. Such activities include efforts to detect, deter, protect against, and, if needed, respond to terrorist attacks."

[103] BCA limits also include separate cap adjustments for program integrity and disaster assistance.

[104] Caps in ATRA were set at $684 billion for defense and $359 billion for nondefense.

[105] For a discussion of defining security or homeland security, see U.S. Congressional Budget Office, "Federal Funding for Homeland Security: An Update," Economic and Budget Issue Brief, July 20, 2005.

[106] CRS Report R42462, *Defining Homeland Security: Analysis and Congressional Considerations*, by Shawn Reese.

[107] U.S. Agency for International Development.

[108] See notes to U.S. Office of Management and Budget, *Budget of the U.S. Government, FY2013*, Tables S-11.

[109] U.S. Office of Management and Budget, *Budget of the U.S. Government, FY2009*, Table S-2.

[110] The Homeland Security Act of 2002 (P.L. 107-296) requires this report, which supersedes a report on anti-terrorism activities mandated by the National Defense Authorization Act of 1998 (P.L. 105-85). An appendix (*Homeland Security Mission Funding by Agency and Budget Account*) is contained in the FY2013 Budget, *Analytical Perspectives* volume, available   at http://www.whitehouse.gov/sites/default/files/omb/budget/fy2013/assets/homeland_supp.pdf.

[111] Funding levels prior to the establishment of Department of Homeland Security (DHS) and National Nuclear Security Administration (NNSA) shown in Figure 7 reflect imputations calculated by OMB or the author. Congress established the DHS in 2003 (P.L. 107-296), which combined dozens of security-related offices under one agency, including the Transportation Security Agency (TSA) to monitor airport security, a new high priority after the 9/11 attacks. DHS began operating on March 1, 2003. The NNSA, which handles nuclear weapon programs within the Energy Department, was established in the FY2000 National Defense Authorization Act (P.L. 106-65, Title XXXII).

[112] Department of Veterans Affairs, "FY2012 Budget Rollout," February 14, 2011.

[113] Spending levels for FY2013-FY2017 reflect the Administration's FY2013 budget proposals.

[114] For a more detailed analysis of spending trends, see CRS Report R41726, *Discretionary Budget Authority by Subfunction: An Overview*, by D. Andrew Austin.

[115] CBO, *Budget Projections—May 2013*, May 14, 2013, available at http://www.cbo.gov/publication/44195.

In: Federal Discretionary Spending ...   ISBN: 978-1-63321-041-7
Editor: Gerald A. Grasso   © 2014 Nova Science Publishers, Inc.

Chapter 2

DISCRETIONARY BUDGET AUTHORITY BY SUBFUNCTION: AN OVERVIEW*

D. Andrew Austin

SUMMARY

This report provides a graphical overview of historical trends in discretionary budget authority (BA) from FY1976 through FY2012, preliminary estimates for FY2013 spending, and the levels consistent with the President's proposals for FY2014 through FY2018 using data from President Obama's FY2014 budget submission that was released on April 10, 2013. Spending caps and budget enforcement mechanisms established in the Budget Control Act of 2011 (P.L. 112-25; BCA) strongly affected the FY2013 and FY2014 budget cycles. Congress modified BCA caps at the beginning of January 2013 to scale down the size of discretionary spending reductions for FY2013 and in December 2013 to scale down the size of reductions slated for FY2014 and FY2015.

As the 113th Congress prepares to consider funding levels for FY2015 and beyond, past spending trends may help frame policy discussions. For example, rapid growth in national defense and other security spending in the past decade has played an important role in fiscal discussions. The

---

* This is an edited, reformatted and augmented version of a Congressional Research Service publication, CRS Report for Congress R41726, prepared for Members and Committees of Congress, from www.crs.gov, dated January 24, 2014.

American Recovery and Reinvestment Act of 2009 (P.L. 111-5; ARRA) funded sharp increases in spending on education, energy, and other areas. Since FY2010, however, base defense discretionary spending has essentially been held flat and non-defense discretionary spending has been reduced significantly. The base defense budget excludes war funding (Overseas Contingency Operations/Global War on Terror). This report provides a starting point for discussions about spending trends. Other CRS products analyze spending trends in specific functional areas.

Functional categories (e.g., national defense, agriculture, etc.) provide a means to compare federal funding for activities within broad policy areas that often cut across several federal agencies. Subfunction categories provide a finer division of funding levels within narrower policy areas. Budget function categories are used within the budget resolution and for other purposes, such as possible program cuts and tax expenditures. Three functions are omitted: (1) allowances, which contain items reflecting technical budget adjustments; (2) net interest, which by its nature is not discretionary spending; and (3) undistributed offsetting receipts, which are treated for federal budgetary purposes as negative budget authority.

Spending in this report is measured and illustrated in terms of discretionary budget authority as a percentage of gross domestic product (GDP). Measuring spending as a percentage of GDP in effect controls for inflation and population increases.

A flat line on such graphs indicates that spending in that category has been increasing at the same rate as overall economic growth. Graphs were updated to reflect the revisions to national income accounts released by the Department of Commerce's Bureau of Economic Analysis in July 2013.

Discretionary spending is provided and controlled through appropriations acts, which provide budget authority to federal agencies to fund many of the activities commonly associated with such federal government functions as running executive branch agencies, congressional offices and agencies, and international operations of the government. Essentially all spending on federal wages and salaries is discretionary.

Program administration costs for entitlement programs such as Social Security are generally funded by discretionary spending, while mandatory spending— not shown in figures presented in this report—generally funds the benefits provided through those programs. For some federal agencies, such as the Departments of Veterans Affairs and Transportation, the division of expenditures into discretionary and mandatory categories can be complex.

INTRODUCTION

This report presents figures showing trends in discretionary budget authority as a percentage of GDP by subfunction within each of 17 budget function categories, using data from President Obama's FY2014 budget submission.[1] This report provides a graphical overview of historical trends in discretionary budget authority from FY1976 through FY2012, preliminary estimates for FY2013 spending, and the levels consistent with the President's proposals for FY2014 through FY2018.[2]

Discretionary spending is provided and controlled through appropriations acts. These acts fund many of the activities commonly associated with federal government functions, such as running executive branch agencies, congressional offices and agencies, and international operations of the government.[3] Thus, the figures showing trends in discretionary budget authority presented below do not reflect the much larger expenditures on program benefits supported by mandatory spending. For some departments, such as Transportation, the division of expenditures into discretionary and mandatory categories can be complex.

Discretionary spending in this report is measured in terms of budget authority. Budget authority for an agency has been compared to having funds in a checking account. Funds are available, subject to congressional restrictions, and can be used to enter into obligations such as contracts or hiring personnel. Outlays occur when the U.S. Treasury disburses funds to honor those obligations. Spending in this report is shown as a percentage of GDP to control for the effects of inflation, population growth, and growth in per capita income. A flat line on such graphs indicates that spending in that category is increasing at the same rate as overall economic growth. Graphs were updated to reflect the revisions to national income accounts released by the Department of Commerce's Bureau of Economic Analysis in July 2013.[4] In general, the revised GDP series showed somewhat higher levels of national income and thus slightly reduced government spending as a share of GDP.

Discussions about the appropriate levels of spending for various policy objectives of the federal government have played an important role in congressional deliberations over funding measures in the last several years and are expected to play a central role as Congress considers decisions affecting the FY2014 budget.[5] As the 113th Congress prepares to consider funding levels for FY2015 and beyond, past spending trends may prove useful in framing policy discussions. For example, rapid growth in national defense and other security spending in the past decade has played an important role in fiscal discussions. The sharp increases in federal spending on education, energy, and other areas funded by the American Recovery and Reinvestment Act of 2009 (P.L. 111-5; ARRA) have also played a significant role in recent budget debates.

Discretionary spending caps and budget enforcement mechanisms established in the Budget Control Act of 2011 (P.L. 112-25; BCA) framed policy discussions during the FY2014 budget cycle.[6] The BCA was signed into law on August 2, 2011, after months of intense negotiations over alternative plans to reduce the deficit and raise the debt limit. In December 2013, the Bipartisan Budget Act (BBA; H.J.Res. 59; P.L. 113-67) modified BCA limits for FY2014 and FY2015. The Consolidated Appropriations Act, 2014 (H.R. 3547; P.L. 113-76), enacted on January 17, 2014, provides funding within those limits for the remainder of FY2014. The BBA also provides top-line defense and non-defense discretionary spending limits for FY2015.

Office of Management and Budget and Federal Budget Data

Figures in this report are based on the Office of Management and Budget (OMB) Public Budget Database accompanying the FY2014 budget release.[7] Table 5.1 in the *Historical Tables* volume of the FY2014 budget reports budget authority by function and subfunction, but does not provide a breakdown by discretionary and mandatory subcomponents.[8]

OMB is the official custodian of historical federal budget data. While OMB has attempted to make these data consistent, changes in government accounting standards and agency reorganizations, among other changes, may raise difficulties in comparing data from different fiscal years. For example, the Department of Homeland Security (DHS) was created in 2002 from 22 existing federal agencies or entities.[9] OMB used historical budget data for those agencies or entities to calculate retrospective estimates for DHS.

Budget data in OMB documents may differ from other budget data for various reasons, although differences in historical data are typically small. For example, appropriations budget documents often reflect scorekeeping adjustments. Budget data issued at a later date may include revisions absent from earlier data. In some cases, detailed appropriations data may differ from OMB data, which sometimes do not reflect certain relatively small zero-balance transfers among funds.

Differences may also reflect technical differences or different interpretations of federal budget concepts.

BACKGROUND ON FUNCTIONAL CATEGORIES

Functional categories provide a means to compare federal funding for activities within broad policy areas that often cut across several federal agencies.[10] Because various federal agencies may have closely related or overlapping responsibilities, and because some agencies have responsibilities in diverse policy areas, budget data divided along functional categories can provide a useful view of federal activities in support of specific national purposes. Superfunction categories, which provide a higher level division of federal activities, are

- National defense,
- Human resources,
- Physical resources, and
- Other functions.

Net interest, Allowances, and Undistributed offsetting receipts could also be considered as separate categories. Superfunction categories for national defense, net interest, allowances, and undistributed offsetting receipts coincide with function categories.

Trends in net interest are excluded as federal interest expenditures have been automatically appropriated since 1847. Allowances, which contain items reflecting technical budget adjustments, and undistributed offsetting receipts, are also excluded. Allowances in FY2014 include unspecified cuts to comply with BCA spending caps, future disaster funding costs, and war funding (Overseas Contingency Operations/OCO; Global War on Terror/GWOT) for years after FY2014.[11]

Budget function categories, grouped by superfunctions, are shown in *Table 1*. Subfunction categories provide a finer division of funding levels within narrower policy areas. Subsequent figures follow the ordering of functions in *Table 1*.

DISCRETIONARY SPENDING IN THE FY2014 BUDGET

Budget discussions for FY2014 in large part were framed by the BCA.[12] Spending limitations on discretionary spending imposed by the BCA had been slated to make sharp reductions in defense and non-defense spending in

FY2013 and FY2014.[13] Congress has modified provisions of the BCA, however, to lessen the stringency of those reductions. Those modifications are discussed in more detail below, after a short explanation of relevant BCA caps.

Table 1. Budget Function Categories by Superfunction

Superfunction	Code	Function / Subfunction
National Defense		
	50	National defense
	51	Dept. of Defense-Military
	53	Atomic energy defense activities
	54	Defense-related activities
Human Resources		
	500	Education, training, employment, and social services
	501	Elementary, secondary, and vocational education
	502	Higher education
	503	Research and general education aids
	504	Training and employment
	505	Other labor services
	506	Social services
	550	Health
	551	Health care services
	552	Health research and training
	554	Consumer and occupational health and safety
	570	Medicare
	571	Medicare
	600	Income security
	601	Gen. retirement & disability insurance (exc. Soc. Sec.)
	602	Federal employee retirement and disability
	603	Unemployment compensation
	604	Housing assistance
	605	Food and nutrition assistance
	609	Other income security
	650	Social security
	651	Social security
	700	Veterans benefits and services
	701	Income security for veterans
	702	Veterans education, training, & rehabilitation
	703	Hospital and medical care for veterans
	704	Veterans housing
	705	Other veterans benefits and services
Physical Resources		
	270	Energy

Superfunction	Code	Function / Subfunction
	271	Energy supply
	272	Energy conservation
	274	Emergency energy preparedness
	276	Energy information, policy, and regulation
	300	Natural resources and environment
	301	Water resources
	302	Conservation and land management
	303	Recreational resources
	304	Pollution control and abatement
	306	Other natural resources
	370	Commerce and housing credit
	371	Mortgage credit
	372	Postal service
	373	Deposit insurance
	376	Other advancement of commerce
	400	Transportation
	401	Ground transportation
	402	Air transportation
	403	Water transportation
	407	Other transportation
	450	Community and regional development
	451	Community development
	452	Area and regional development
	453	Disaster relief and insurance
Other Functions		
	150	International affairs
	151	Intl. dev. and humanitarian assistance
	152	Intl. security assistance
	153	Conduct of foreign affairs
	154	Foreign information & exchange activities
	155	Intl. financial programs
	250	General science, space, and technology
	251	General science and basic research
	252	Space flight, research & supporting activities
	350	Agriculture
	351	Farm income stabilization
	352	Agricultural research and services
	750	Administration of justice
	751	Federal law enforcement activities
	752	Federal litigative and judicial activities
	753	Federal correctional activities
	754	Criminal justice assistance

Table 1. (Continued)

Superfunction	Code	Function / Subfunction
	800	General government
	801	Legislative functions
	802	Executive direction and mgmt.
	803	Central fiscal operations
	804	General property and records mgmt.
	805	Central personnel mgmt.
	806	General purpose fiscal assistance
	808	Other general government
	809	Deductions for offsetting receipts
Net Interest		
	900	Net interest
	901	Interest on Treasury debt securities (gross)
	902	Interest received by on-budget trust funds
	903	Interest received by off-budget trust funds
	908	Other interest
	909	Other Investment and income
Allowances		
	920	Allowances
	921	Adjustment for BCA Cap on Security Spending
	924	Adjustment for BCA Cap on Non-Security Spending
	925	Future Disaster Costs
	929	Plug for Outyear War Costs
Undistributed Offsetting Receipts		
	950	Undistributed offsetting receipts
	951	Employer share, employee retirement (on-budget)
	952	Employer share, employee retirement (off-budget)
	953	Rents & royalties on the Outer Continental Shelf
	954	Sale of major assets
	959	Other undistributed offsetting receipts

Source: CRS, based on OMB data.
Note: Allowances subfunctions often change from one year to the next.

Caps Lowered in Absence of Super Committee Plan

When the Joint Select Committee on Deficit Reduction (JSC), known as the "Super Committee," did not present a plan to achieve at least $1.2 trillion in deficit reduction over FY2013-FY2021, the original BCA caps were then

superseded by *revised caps*, which imposed separate limits on base defense (budget function 050) and non-defense spending. Base defense funding covers normal costs of national defense, while war costs are not subject to BCA caps.[14] The sum of total discretionary spending under the original and revised caps was the same. Further reductions of $109 billion for each year from the revised cap levels, split between defense and non-defense, were slated to occur in each year from FY2013 through FY2021. In FY2013 savings were to be made through sequestration, and in years FY2014-FY2021 savings are slated to occur through a lowering of the discretionary spending caps. Those lowered caps, along with interest savings and an ongoing sequester of non-exempt mandatory spending, were designed to capture the $1.2 trillion in budget savings in the absence of a Super Committee plan.

Fiscal Cliff Deal and the American Taxpayer Relief Act

The American Taxpayer Relief Act (H.R. 8; P.L. 112-240; ATRA) delayed the Super Committee sequester by two months, from January 2, 2013, to March 1, 2013.[15] In addition, the size of the FY2013 sequestration cuts was reduced from $109 billion to $85 billion.[16] Discretionary caps on FY2014 defense and non-defense funding, as part of an offset for that reduction, were reduced by $4 billion each. Thus, the revised cap on FY2014 defense funding was reduced from $556 billion to $552 billion. The revised cap on FY2014 non-defense funding was reduced from $510 billion to $506 billion. Defense and non-defense spending are slated for reductions of $54.7 billion each, allocated between discretionary and mandatory spending. Because non-exempt defense mandatory spending is relatively small, most of the defense reduction would be borne by base defense discretionary spending via a lowered cap. According to preliminary OMB estimates, the lowered FY2014 cap for base defense discretionary BA will be $468.8 billion.[17]

On the non-defense side for FY2014, Medicare patient care expenses and other non-exempt mandatory spending were estimated to bear $18.1 billion of the $54.7 billion reduction through a sequester, according to OMB. The remaining $36.6 billion would be borne by non-defense discretionary spending via a lowering of its revised cap ($506 billion) to $469.4 billion.[18]

The FY2013 Super Committee sequester, implemented on March 1, 2013, reduced Medicare mandatory patient care spending by $11.3 billion and other non-defense mandatory spending by $5.4 billion, while non-defense discretionary BA was reduced by $25.8 billion.[19] The reduction that had been

slated for non-defense in FY2014 was larger than the FY2013 reductions for two reasons. First, the non-defense sequester was half of $85 billion, rather than the half of $109 billion sequester slated for FY2014. Second, the reduction of Medicare patient care spending is limited to 2%, which implies that changes in the size of non-defense reductions will be chiefly reflected in changes in funding of discretionary programs and non-exempt non-Medicare mandatory programs.[20]

FY2014 Administration Proposals Regarding Caps

The Administration in its FY2014 budget, submitted on April 10, 2013, proposed a set of modifications of BCA caps on discretionary spending. The Administration proposed that FY2014 spending limits be set at revised cap levels (i.e., $552 billion for defense and $506 billion for nondefense) rather than lowered cap levels (i.e., $498.1 billion for defense and $469.4 billion for non-defense), which would have allowed higher levels of discretionary spending while the economy is still recovering from a major recession. Spending limits for the second half of the FY2013-FY2021 budget window, in the Administration's proposals, would have been lowered by $60 billion apiece for defense and non-defense. In addition, discretionary caps would have been extended to FY2022 and FY2023.

The Administration estimated that those spending cap modifications would reduce discretionary spending by $202 billion over the FY2014-FY2023.[21] Thus, projected discretionary spending for FY2014-FY2018 shown in the figures below, which presume the President's budgetary proposals are adopted, reflects an assumption that BCA constraints on discretionary spending would be loosened in FY2014 and tightened later on starting in FY2017. The Administration's FY2014 budget plan also includes $260 billion in unspecified reductions in discretionary spending, mostly slated for FY2015 through FY2023.[22] If those reductions were carried out, discretionary spending levels would have been less than that shown in figures below.

The Bipartisan Budget Act of 2013

During the FY2014 budget cycle, the House and Senate responded to the budgetary challenges presented by BCA caps in different ways. Just before the August 2013 recess, the gap between House and Senate totals for FY2014

discretionary spending stood at about $90 billion. The House Appropriations Committee set suballocations for its subcommittees that totaled $973.1 billion, slightly above total discretionary spending at BCA lowered caps levels ($967.5 billion) for FY2014.[23] Senate Appropriations Committee guidance for its subcommittees, however, indicated a total for FY2014 consistent with BCA revised caps (i.e., a total of $1,058 billion split between a base defense subtotal of $552 billion and a non-defense total of $506 billion).[24]

Differences between House and Senate discretionary spending levels were not resolved before the start of FY2014 on October 1, 2013, which resulted in a shutdown of most federal operations.[25] Funding for federal operations was restored by passage of a continuing resolution (H.R. 2775) on October 16, 2013, which was signed by the President the following morning (Continuing Appropriations Act, 2014; P.L. 113-46). The measure provides funding on an annualized basis of $986.3 billion before adjustments.[26]

The Bipartisan Budget Act of 2013 (H.J.Res. 59; P.L. 113-67) provided a reconciliation of House and Senate discretionary spending levels for the remainder of FY2014 and for FY2015 as well. The discretionary defense spending caps were set at $520.464 billion for FY2014 and $521.272 billion for FY2015. Non-defense caps were set at $491.773 billion for FY2014 and $492.356 billion for FY2015.[27] The mechanism for reducing the revised BCA caps to lowered caps levels in order to capture savings not attained by the Joint Select Committee on Deficit Reduction was turned off for both FY2014 and FY2015.[28] Both modified defense and non-defense spending limits for FY2014 were $22.4 billion above the lowered caps levels that would have applied in the absence of the Bipartisan Budget Act, while FY2015 levels were about $9 billion higher.[29]

Final Appropriations for FY2014

On January 13, 2013, the House and Senate Appropriations Committees announced agreement on an appropriations measure that would provide funding for the remainder of FY2014 within the limits set by the Bipartisan Budget Act. The agreement was incorporated into a Senate amendment to H.R. 3547, retitled as the Consolidated Appropriations Act, 2014 (P.L. 113-76). The House approved the measure on January 14, 2014, on a 359-67 vote and the Senate passed it on a 72-26 vote the following day. The President then signed the act on January 17, 2014.

DISCRETIONARY
CAPS AND SPENDING TRENDS

Discretionary spending as a share of GDP, if modified BCA caps remain in place, will decline to levels well below that seen in recent decades. In real dollar terms (i.e., adjusting for inflation but not for growth in population or the economy), discretionary base defense spending would revert to a level slightly above its FY2007 level, while non-defense discretionary spending would revert a level near its 2002 level.[30] In later years, BCA caps would allow for modest growth in nominal (i.e., not adjusted for inflation) terms. By contrast, mandatory spending and net interest costs are projected to rise, implying that discretionary spending's share of total federal spending would continue to fall.

Actual discretionary budget authority totals will differ from BCA discretionary caps because some types of spending are not subject to caps, such as war spending, certain amounts of disaster relief assistance, and program integrity initiatives.[31] In addition, scorekeeping adjustments typically lead to differences between scored totals of budget authority used to check conformity to BCA spending limits and other budget totals that do not include those adjustments.

Negative Budget Authority

Within the federal budget concepts, certain inflows, such as offsetting receipts, offsetting collections, some user fees, and "profits" from federal loan programs, are treated as negative budget authority.[32] The federal government uses a modified form of accrual accounting for loan and loan guarantee programs since passage of the Federal Credit Reform Act (FCRA) as well as for certain federal retirement programs.[33]

OMB calculates net subsidy rates according to FCRA rules for loan and loan guarantee programs. In some cases, FCRA calculations yield negative net subsidy levels, implying that the federal government appears to make a profit on those loans.[34] FCRA subsidy calculations, however, omit risk adjustments.[35]

The true economic cost of federal credit guarantees can be substantially underestimated when risk adjustments are omitted.[36]

HISTORICAL SPENDING TRENDS

Federal spending trends in functional areas are affected by changing assessments of national priorities, evolving international challenges, and economic conditions, as well as changing social characteristics and demographics of the U.S. population. Some of the trends and events that have had dramatic effects on federal spending are outlined below. Other CRS products provide background on more specific policy areas.

Cold War, Peace Dividend, and the Global War on Terror

The allocation of discretionary spending between defense and non-defense programs is one reflection of changing federal priorities over time. *Figure 1* shows defense and non-defense discretionary funding as a percentage of GDP. *Figure 2* shows subfunctions within the National Defense (050) budget function. The Department of Defense (DOD)-Military subfunction accounts for over 95% of funding within that budget function.

Relations between the United States and its allies on one hand, and the Union of Soviet Socialist Republics (USSR) and its allies on the other were the dominant security concern in the half century following the Second World War. In the early 1970s, U.S. involvement in the Vietnam War wound down, while the United States and the USSR moved towards detente, permitting a thaw in Cold War relations between the two superpowers and a reduction in defense spending relative to the size of the economy.[37]

Following intervention by the USSR in Afghanistan in 1979, military spending increased sharply.[38] Defense spending continued to increase until 1986, as concern shifted to domestic priorities and the need to reduce large budget deficits. The collapse in 1989 of most of the Warsaw Pact governments in Central and Eastern Europe and the 1990-1991 disintegration of the Soviet Union was followed by a reduction in federal defense spending, allowing a "peace dividend" that relaxed fiscal pressures.[39]

The attacks on the World Trade Center towers in New York City and on the Pentagon on September 11, 2001, were followed by sharp increases in homeland security spending. Defense spending also increased dramatically with the start of the Afghanistan war in October 2001 and the Iraq war in March 2003.[40] U.S. combat troops were withdrawn from Iraq in December 2011, and President Obama has announced that most U.S. troops would be withdrawn from Afghanistan by the end of 2014.[41]

Spending on non-defense security spending also rose after the attacks of September 11, 2001, as the federal government overhauled airport security procedures, and then established the Department of Homeland Security. In 2005, hurricanes Katrina and Rita led to a spike in disaster relief spending.[42] Non-security spending also rose to fund new initiatives in education and in other areas.[43]

In 2007, a severe credit crunch affected global financial markets, which led to a fully fledged financial crisis in 2008 and a severe economic recession. The American Recovery and Reinvestment Act of 2009 (P.L. 111-5; ARRA), designed to stimulate the economy and prevent further slowing of economic activity, sharply increased federal spending on education, energy, and support for state and local governments. ARRA also included broad tax cuts through a Making Work Pay credit and other provisions. The decline in federal revenues and the increase in spending caused the deficit to treble from $459 billion in FY2008 to $1.4 trillion in FY2009.

Since FY2010, base defense discretionary spending has been held flat and non-defense discretionary spending has been reduced significantly.[44] The BCA, as noted above, reimposed discretionary spending limits that are slated to remain in place until FY2021.

The Recovery Act

After the financial crisis of 2007-2008 plunged the United States in the deepest economic recession in decades, Congress passed the American Recovery and Reinvestment Act of 2009 (P.L. 111-5; ARRA), often known as the Recovery Act. ARRA includes support for state and local governments in the form of increased infrastructure, Medicaid, school funding, funding for health care IT, extended unemployment benefits, as well as tax cuts and rebates among other provisions.[45] According to initial CBO estimates, ARRA provisions were expected to total $787.2 billion in increased spending and reduced taxes over the FY2009-FY2019 period or just over 5% of GDP in 2008, while a more recent CBO estimate put the total at $814 billion.[46]

The effects of Recovery Act spending can be seen in *Figure 3,* where pronounced increases in education, training, employment, and social services subfunctions can be seen for FY2009. Smaller increases can be seen in *Figure 9,* which shows energy subfunctions, and in *Figure 10,* which shows natural resources and environment subfunctions.

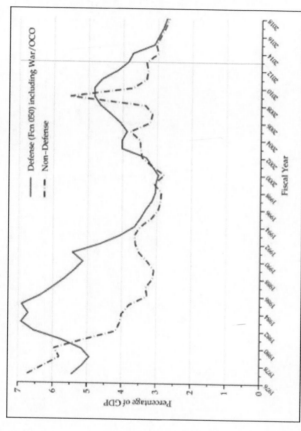

Source: CRS analysis of OMB data.

Notes: Defense is defined as funding for the National Defense (050) budget function; non-defense is the remainder. FY1976-FY2012 are historical data; FY2013 is estimated; FY2014-FY2018 reflect the President's FY2014 budget proposals. This figure assumes unspecified cuts to meet BCA caps are borne by non-defense programs. See text for other important caveats.

Figure 1. Discretionary Defense and Non-Defense Spending, FY1976-FY2018. (Budget authority as a percentage of GDP).

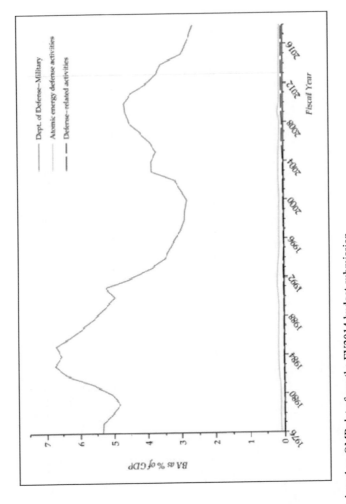

Source: CRS, based on OMB data from the FY2014 budget submission
Notes: FY2014-FY2018 levels reflect Administration proposals and projections. See OMB budget documents for further caveats.

Figure 2. National Defense (050) Subfunctions. (Discretionary budget authority as a percentage of GDP, FY1976-FY2018).

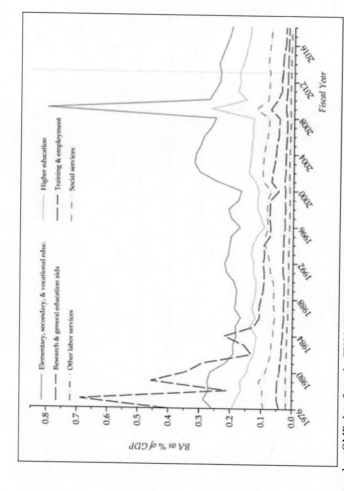

Source: CRS, based on OMB data from the FY2014 budget submission.

Notes: FY2014-FY2018 levels reflect Administration proposals and projections. See OMB budget documents for further caveats.

Figure 3. Education, Training, Employment, and Social Services (500) Subfunctions. (Discretionary budget authority as a percentage of GDP, FY1976-FY2018).

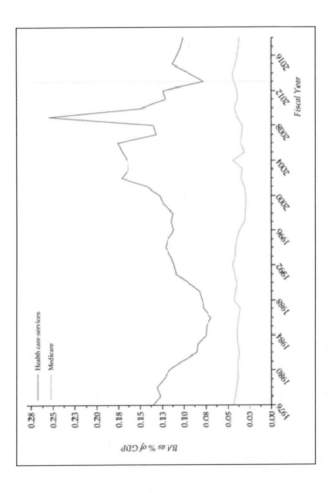

Source: CRS, based on OMB data from the FY2014 budget submission.

Notes: FY2014-FY2018 levels reflect Administration proposals and projections. Discretionary BA for Medicare funds program administration, and does not generally fund program benefits. See OMB budget documents for further caveats.

Figure 4. Health Care Services (Subfunction 551) and Medicare (Subfunction 571). (Discretionary budget authority as a percentage of GDP, FY1976-FY2018).

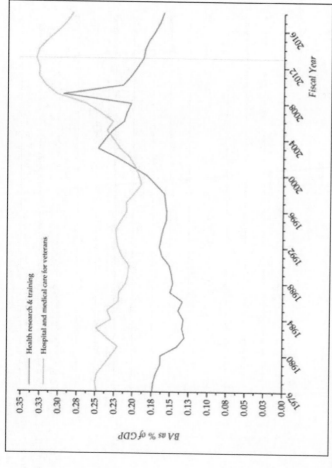

Source: CRS, based on OMB data from the FY2014 budget submission.

Notes: Hospital and medical care for veterans (703) presented here for comparison and also appears in Figure 9. FY2014-FY2018 levels reflect Administration proposals and projections. See OMB budget documents for further caveats.

Figure 5. Smaller Health Subfunctions. (Discretionary budget authority as a percentage of GDP, FY1976-FY2018).

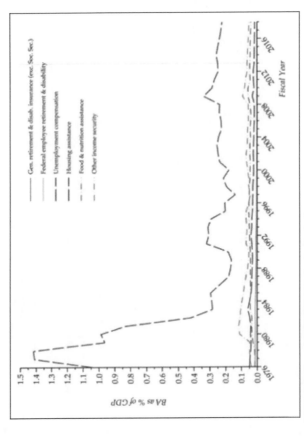

Source: CRS, based on OMB data from the FY2014 budget submission.
Notes: Discretionary funding for income security programs supports program administration; most income security benefits are generally funded by mandatory spending, which is not shown here. FY2014-FY2018 levels reflect Administration proposals and projections. See OMB budget documents for further caveats.

Figure 6. Income Security (600) Subfunctions. (Discretionary budget authority as a percentage of GDP, FY1976-FY2018).

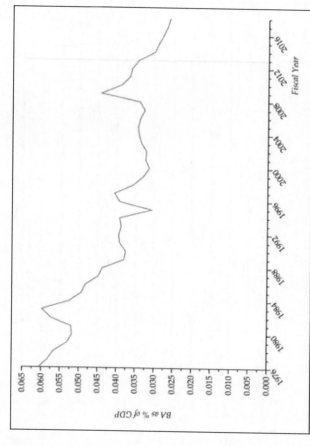

Source: CRS, based on OMB data from the FY2014 budget submission.

Notes: Discretionary funding for Social Security supports program administration; Social Security benefits are generally funded by mandatory spending, which is not shown here. FY2014-FY2018 levels reflect Administration proposals and projections. See OMB budget documents for further caveats.

Figure 7. Social Security (650) Subfunction. (Discretionary budget authority as a percentage of GDP, FY1976-FY2018).

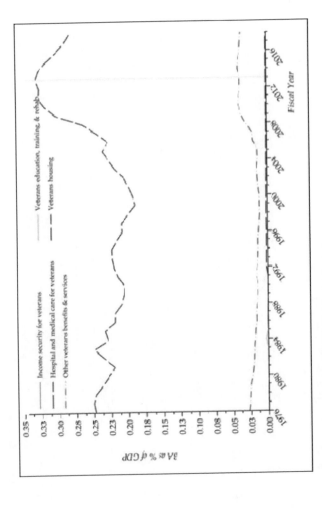

Source: CRS, based on OMB data from the FY2014 budget submission.
Notes: FY2014-FY2018 levels reflect Administration proposals and projections. See OMB budget documents for further caveats. Note that mandatory Veterans Affairs expenditures, which chiefly support income security programs, are not reflected here.

Figure 8. Veterans Benefits and Services (700) Subfunctions. (Discretionary budget authority as a percentage of GDP, FY1976-FY2018).

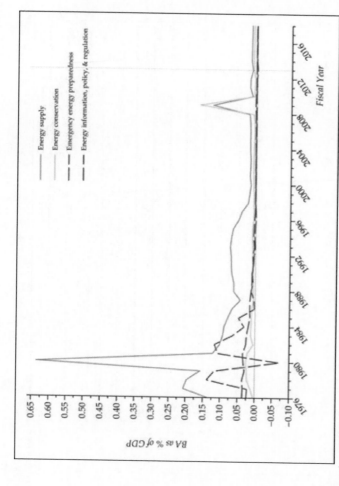

Source: CRS, based on OMB data from FY2014 budget submission.

Notes: FY2014-FY2018 levels reflect Administration proposals and projections. See OMB budget documents for further caveats.

Figure 9. Energy (270) Subfunctions. (Discretionary budget authority as a percentage of GDP, FY1976-FY2018).

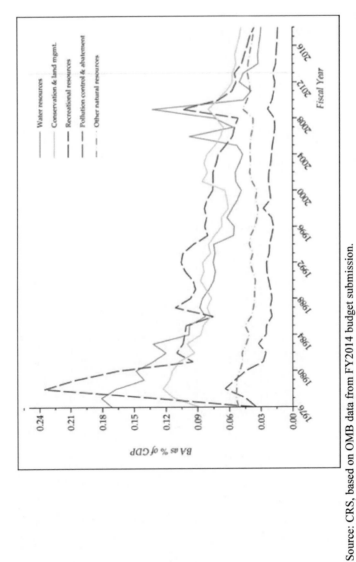

Source: CRS, based on OMB data from FY2014 budget submission.
Notes: FY2014-FY2018 levels reflect Administration proposals and projections. See OMB budget documents for further caveats.

Figure 10. Natural Resources and Environment (300) Subfunctions. (Discretionary budget authority as a percentage of GDP, FY1976-FY2018).

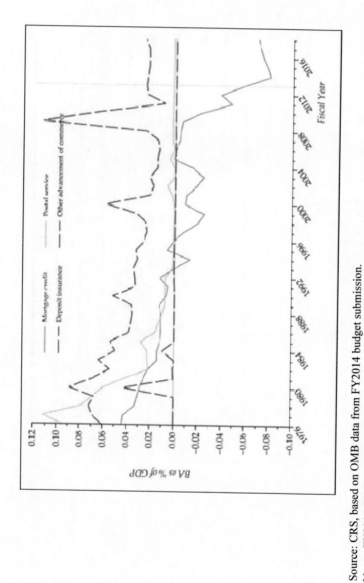

Source: CRS, based on OMB data from FY2014 budget submission.
Notes: FY2014-FY2018 levels reflect Administration proposals and projections. See OMB budget documents for further caveats.

Figure 11. Commerce and Housing Credit Subfunctions. (Discretionary budget authority as a percentage of GDP, FY1976-FY2018).

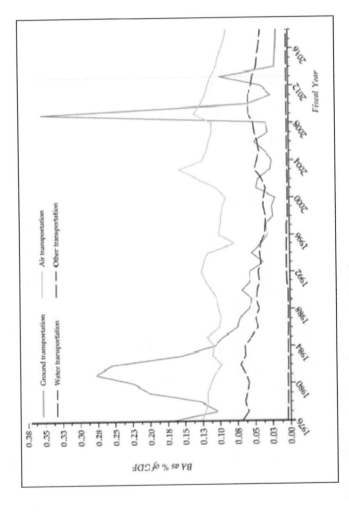

Source: CRS, based on OMB data from FY2014 budget submission.
Notes: FY2014-FY2018 levels reflect Administration proposals and projections. See OMB budget documents for further caveats.

Figure 12. Transportation (400) Subfunctions. (Discretionary budget authority as a percentage of GDP, FY1976-FY2018).

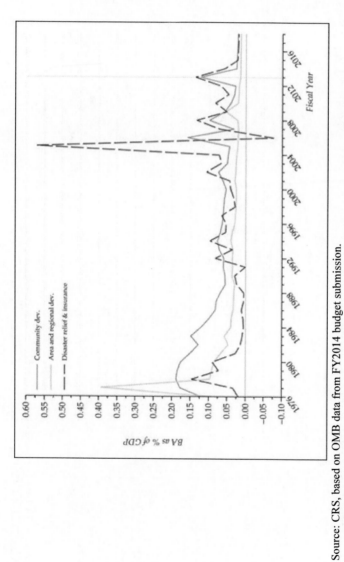

Source: CRS, based on OMB data from FY2014 budget submission.
Notes: FY2014-FY2018 levels reflect Administration proposals and projections. See OMB budget documents for further caveats.

Figure 13. Community and Regional Development (450) Subfunctions. (Discretionary budget authority as a percentage of GDP, FY1976-FY2018).

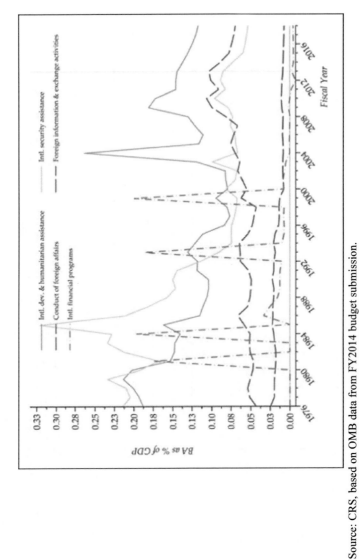

Source: CRS, based on OMB data from FY2014 budget submission.

Notes: FY2014-FY2018 levels reflect Administration proposals and projections. See OMB budget documents for further caveats.

Figure 14. International Affairs (150) Subfunctions. (Discretionary budget authority as a percentage of GDP, FY1976-FY2018).

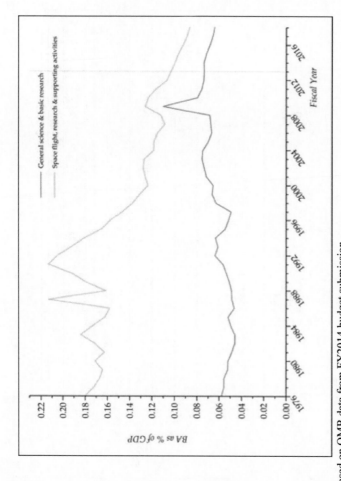

Source: CRS, based on OMB data from FY2014 budget submission.

Notes: FY2014-FY2018 levels reflect Administration proposals and projections. See OMB budget documents for further caveats.

Figure 15. General Science, Space, and Technology (250) Subfunctions. (Discretionary budget authority as a percentage of GDP, FY1976-FY2018).

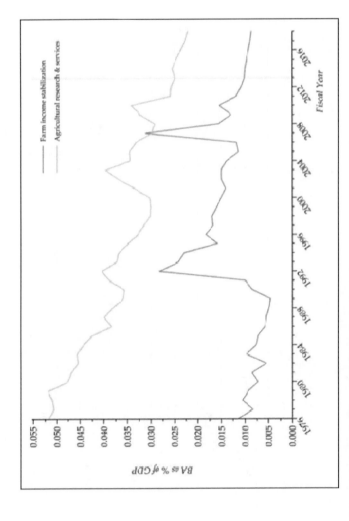

Source: CRS, based on OMB data from FY2014 budget submission.
Notes: FY2014-FY2018 levels reflect Administration proposals and projections. See OMB budget documents for further caveats.

Figure 16. Agriculture (350) Subfunctions. (Discretionary budget authority as a percentage of GDP, FY1976-FY2018).

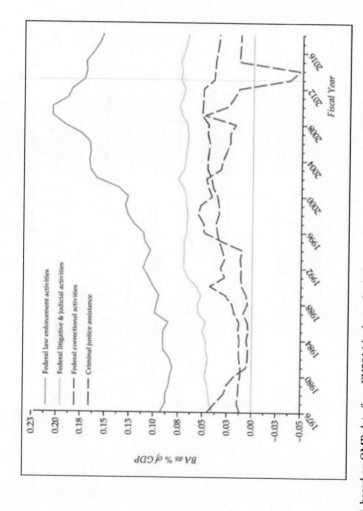

Source: CRS, based on OMB data from FY2014 budget submission.

Notes: FY2014-FY2018 levels reflect Administration proposals and projections. See OMB budget documents for further caveats.

Figure 17. Administration of Justice (750) Subfunctions. (Discretionary budget authority as a percentage of GDP, FY1976-FY2018).

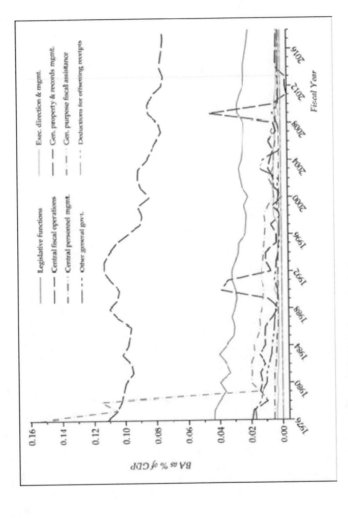

Source: CRS, based on OMB data from FY2014 budget submission.
Notes: FY2014-FY2018 levels reflect Administration proposals and projections. See OMB budget documents for further caveats.

Figure 18. General Government (800) Subfunctions. (Discretionary budget authority as a percentage of GDP, FY1976-FY2018).

Federal Health Programs

Costs of federal health programs continue to play a central role in budgetary discussions. The costs of the largest federal health programs, Medicare and the federal portion of Medicaid costs, are nearly all mandatory. Administrative costs, which account for a small portion of those costs, are nearly all funded as discretionary spending. Federal health research and veterans' health care is mostly funded through discretionary spending, as are certain public health clinics. Trends in funding of health subfunctions are shown in two separate figures. Larger programs (health care services/subfunction 551 and Medicare/function 570/subfunction 571) are shown in *Figure 4*, and smaller programs (health research and training/subfunction 552 and consumer and occupational health and safety/subfunction 554) are shown in *Figure 5*.

The National Institutes of Health (NIH) are the largest part of the health research and training subfunction. Veterans' health programs, which fall under the veterans benefits and services function, are also shown in *Figure 8* to make comparisons among those programs easier.

End Notes

[1] The President's FY2014 budget was released on April 10, 2013, and is available at http://www.whitehouse.gov/omb/ budget/.

[2] The start of the federal fiscal year was changed from July 1 to October 1 in 1976 to accommodate changes in the congressional budget process. The figures omit data for the transition quarter (July 1 to September 30, 1976). It appears that FY2013 data omit the effects related to the March 1, 2013, sequestration triggered by the absence of a Joint Select Committee on Deficit Reduction (Super Committee) plan and final action on FY2013 appropriations. See FY2014 Budget of the U.S. Government, Summary Table S-4, note 2.

[3] For a broader analysis of discretionary spending, see CRS Report RL34424, Trends in Discretionary Spending, by D. Andrew Austin.

[4] The Bureau of Economic Analysis (BEA) has provided extensive technical information on its revision of national income and product accounts (NIPA), which is available here: http://bea.gov/national/an1.htm#2013comprehensive. The revision, according to BEA, included several major improvements to the accounts, including expanded capitalization of intellectual property products and a change to accrual accounting for defined benefit pension plans. The revision covered estimates from 1929 through the first quarter of 2013. For 2002–2012, the revised estimate of average annual economic growth is 1.8%, or 0.2 percentage points higher than previously published estimates. For years 2009–2012, the revised estimate of annual economic growth is 2.4%, or 0.3 percentage points higher than previously published estimates. For details see Stephanie H. McCulla, Alyssa E. Holdren, and Shelly Smith, "Improved Estimates of the National Income and Product Accounts:

Results of the 2013 Comprehensive Revision," Survey of Current Business, September 2013, pp. 14-45; available at http://bea.gov/scb/pdf/2013/09%20September/ 0913_compre hensive_nipa_revision.pdf.

[5] CRS Report R41771, FY2011 Appropriations in Budgetary Context, by D. Andrew Austin and Amy Belasco.

[6] CRS Report R41965, The Budget Control Act of 2011, by Bill Heniff Jr., Elizabeth Rybicki, and Shannon M. Mahan.

[7] Data in the OMB Public Budget Database reconcile to information presented in the Historical Tables volume of the FY2014 budget. The Public Budget Database itself is available here: http://www.whitehouse.gov/omb/budget/ Supplemental. For a further description and important caveats, see the Public Budget Database User Guide, available at http://www. whitehouse.gov/sites/default/files/omb/budget/fy2014/assets/db_guide.pdf.

[8] Table 5.1 of the OMB Historical Tables is available at http://www.whitehouse. gov/sites/default/files/omb/budget/ fy2014/assets/hist05z1.xls.

[9] Department of Homeland Security, "Creation of the Department of Homeland Security," available at http://www.dhs.gov/creation-department-homeland-security.

[10] For further background on functional categories, see CRS Report 98-280, Functional Categories of the Federal Budget, by Bill Heniff Jr.

[11] The allowance for future disaster costs is not included in calculations underlying graphs in order to conform with published data aggregates. Allowances that reflect enforcement of BCA discretionary spending limits are not included, as they are not disaggregated by function.

[12] Budget Control Act of 2011 (P.L. 112-25; BCA).

[13] For a more complete description of recent budget legislation, see CRS Report RL34424, Trends in Discretionary Spending, by D. Andrew Austin.

[14] War costs, however, are not exempt from sequestration. Those costs are described as Overseas Contingency Operations (OCO) in budget documents.

[15] For details, see CRS Report R42949, The American Taxpayer Relief Act of 2012: Modifications to the Budget Enforcement Procedures in the Budget Control Act, by Bill Heniff Jr. ATRA was sent to the President on January 1, 2013, and enacted the following day.

[16] Thus the size of the FY2013 sequester was reduced by $24 billion.

[17] OMB, Sequestration Preview Report to the President and Congress for FY2014 (corrected May 20, 2013), Tables 1 and 3, available at http://www.whitehouse.gov/sites/default/files/ omb/assets/legislative_reports/fy14_preview_and_joint_committee_reductions_reports_052 02013.pdf.

[18] Ibid., Table 3, p. 15.

[19] The BCA specifies sequester reductions in mandatory spending in terms of outlays. For discretionary spending, the Super Committee sequester canceled budget authority for FY2013. Discretionary spending reductions are slated to be implemented through lowered caps on budget authority from FY2014 through FY2021. See OMB, Report to the Congress on the Joint Committee Sequestration for Fiscal Year 2013, March 1, 2013; available at http://www.whitehouse.gov/sites/default/files/omb/assets/legislative_reports/fy13ombjcsequ estrationreport.pdf.

[20] The reduction in Medicare patient care spending is accomplished by a 2% reduction in provider payments, which are considered payment in full.

[21] OMB, FY2014 Budget of the U.S. Government, p. 45. See Table 6 of memorandum cited below for $800 billion estimate for difference between BCA revised caps and lowered caps.

[22] According to the FY2014 Mid Session Review, "(t)he 2014 Budget includes allowances, similar to the Function 920 allowances used in Budget Resolutions, to represent amounts to be allocated among the respective agencies to reach the proposed defense and non-defense caps for 2015 and beyond. These levels are determined for illustrative purposes but do not reflect specific policy decisions." See fn. 5, to Table S-10, p. 58; available at http://www.whitehouse.gov/sites/ default/files/omb/budget/fy2014/assets/14msr.pdf.

[23] See CBO, "FY 2014 House Current Status of Discretionary Appropriations as of August 1, 2013," available at http://www.cbo.gov/sites/default/files/cbofiles/attachments/44333_BY2014House_8-1.pdf and OMB Sequestration Preview Report (cited above). CBO estimated that the Homeland Security bill would include a $5.6 billion disaster funding adjustment.

[24] That Senate total excluded adjustments to caps for war funding (OCO), disaster funding, program integrity, and emergency items. With those adjustments, the Senate total for FY2014 appropriations at the end of July 2013 was $1,149.6 billion. See CBO, "FY 2014 Senate Current Status of Discretionary Appropriations as of August 2, 2013," available at http://www.cbo.gov/sites/default/files/cbofiles/attachments/44399_BY2014_Senate_8-2.pdf.

[25] For details, see CRS Report R43338, Congressional Action on FY2014 Appropriations Measures, by Jessica Tollestrup.

[26] That total excludes adjustments for war funding (OCO), disaster funding, program integrity, and emergency items. Annualized funding reflecting those adjustments totaled $1,087.7 billion. See CBO, "CBO Estimate of the Continuing Appropriations Act, 2014, as Introduced in the Senate on October 16, 2013, as an Amendment to H.R. 2775," October 16, 2013; available at http://www.cbo.gov/sites/default/files/cbofiles/attachments/ContinuingAppropriationsAct2014.pdf.

[27] The defense category (i.e., the National Defense budget function (050)) is called the "revised security category" in the BCA and the Bipartisan Budget Act of 2013. The non-defense category is called the "revised nonsecurity category."

[28] BBEDCA Section 251A (2 U.S.C. 901a) directs OMB to lower the revised spending caps for FY2014-FY2021. Section 101 of the Bipartisan Budget Act of 2013 requires that the lowering of caps "shall not be implemented for fiscal years 2014 and 2015."

[29] CRS calculations based on CBO and OMB data.

[30] For details, see CRS, "The Budget Control Act and Alternate Defense and Non-Defense Spending Paths, FY2012- FY2021," by Amy Belasco and Andrew Austin, November 16, 2012, available from authors. This comparison is made in terms of budget authority. Before passage of ATRA, BCA provisions were slated to bring discretionary base defense spending to its FY2007 level and non-defense spending to near its level in FY2003 or FY2004. Inflation adjustments made using GDP price index.

[31] Those caps are adjusted upwards to reflect those spending categories, within specified limits.

[32] See OMB, FY2014 Budget, Analytic Perspectives, ch. 11, "Budget Concepts." In particular, pp. 117-122 cover these topics.

[33] See out-of-print CRS Report RL30346, Federal Credit Reform: Implementation of the Changed Budgetary Treatment of Direct Loans and Loan Guarantees, by James M. Bickley, available upon request.

[34] For example, some Federal Housing Administration mortgage programs and some federal student loan programs have been estimated to yield negative net subsidies.

[35] While the FCRA calculations include estimates of default costs, they do not discount more volatile income flows, as a private firm would.

[36] U.S. Congressional Budget Office, Estimating the Value of Subsidies for Federal Loans and Loan Guarantees, August 2004, available at http://cbo.gov/doc.cfm?index=5751. CBO and OMB include risk adjustments in estimates of the costs associated with the TARP as mandated by the Emergency Economic Stabilization Act of 2008 (P.L. 110-343; EESA). See U.S. Congressional Budget Office, The Budget and Economic Outlook: Fiscal Years 2009 to 2019, January 7, 2009, pp. 25-26, available at http://www.cbo.gov/ftpdocs/99xx/doc9957/01-07-Outlook.pdf; Testimony of Elizabeth Warren, Chair of the Congressional Oversight Panel, in Congress, Senate Banking Committee, Pulling Back the TARP: Oversight of the Financial Rescue Program, hearings, 111th Congress, 1st sess., February 5, 2009, available at http://banking.senate.gov/public/_files/Warrentestimonyfinal 2509.pdf.

[37] For a history of deficit finance and American wars, see Robert D. Hormats, The Price of Liberty, (New York: Times Books, 2007). Also see CRS Report RL31176, Financing Issues and Economic Effects of American Wars, by Marc Labonte and Mindy R. Levit.

[38] For one view of budgetary politics in the early 1980s, see David Stockman, The Triumph of Politics, (New York: Harper & Row, 1986).

[39] The Warsaw Treaty Organization, established in 1955, included Albania, Bulgaria, Czechoslovakia, the German Democratic Republic, Hungary, Poland, Romania, and the Soviet Union.

[40] CRS Report RL33110, The Cost of Iraq, Afghanistan, and Other Global War on Terror Operations Since 9/11, by Amy Belasco. The Afghan and Iraq wars, along with other related activities, are often called the Global War on Terror (GWOT).

[41] See CRS Report RL30588, Afghanistan: Post-Taliban Governance, Security, and U.S. Policy, by Kenneth Katzman.

[42] See CRS Report R40708, Disaster Relief Funding and Supplemental Appropriations for Disaster Relief, by Bruce R. Lindsay and Justin Murray.

[43] The Obama Administration defined security spending in its FY2012 budget as funding for Department of Defense-Military (subfunction 051); the Department of Energy's National Nuclear Security Administration; International Affairs (function 150, which includes State Department and related agencies); the Department of Homeland Security; and the Department of Veterans Affairs. The BCA defined security similarly, except that it included all military activities within the Department of Defense excluding war funding (i.e., defined by department rather than by subfunction), and also included the Intelligence Community Management Account.

[44] The base defense budget excludes war funding (Overseas Contingency Operations).

[45] For more information on the provisions of ARRA, see CRS Report R40537, American Recovery and Reinvestment Act of 2009 (P.L. 111-5): Summary and Legislative History, by Clinton T. Brass et al.

[46] For initial estimates, see U.S. Congressional Budget Office, Cost Estimate For the Conference Agreement For H.R. 1, February 13, 2009, available at http://cbo.gov/ftpdocs/99xx/doc9989/hr1conference.pdf. For a later assessment, see CBO, Budget and Economic Outlook: An Update, August 2010, Box 1-2, available at http://www.cbo.gov/ftpdocs/117xx/doc11705/08-18-Update.pdf.

INDEX